THE SCENTED ROOM

Barbara Milo Ohrbach

The Scented Room

CHERCHEZ'S® BOOK OF DRIED FLOWERS, FRAGRANCE, AND POTPOURRI

Photographs by Joe Standart   Text with Anne Marie Cloutier

Clarkson N. Potter, Inc./Publishers
DISTRIBUTED BY CROWN PUBLISHERS, INC.   NEW YORK

Designed by Rochelle Udell and Douglas Turshen

Copyright © 1986 by Barbara Milo Ohrbach

Published by Clarkson N. Potter, Inc., 225 Park Avenue South, New York, New York 10003, and represented in Canada by the Canadian Manda Group

CLARKSON N. POTTER, POTTER, and colophon are trademarks of Clarkson N. Potter, Inc.

Manufactured in Japan

Library of Congress Cataloging-in-Publication Data

Ohrbach, Barbara Milo.
The scented room.

Bibliography: p.   Includes index.
1. Flowers—Drying.   2. Dried flower arrangement.   3. Aromatic plants.
4. Flowers—Odors.
I. Cloutier, Anne Marie.   II. Standart, Joe.
III. Cherchez (Firm).   IV. Title.
SB449.3.D7047 1986   745.92   85–30020

ISBN 0-517-56081-X
10 9 8 7 6 5 4

For my mother,
whose sunny disposition
and cheerful optimism
always created a perfect climate
for people and flowers to grow in,
and for my little nephew Harry,
who seems to be following in
her footsteps

ACKNOWLEDGMENTS

The making of a book takes the time, co-operation, and knowledge of so very many people. My deep appreciation to everyone who helped, especially—

My editor, Carolyn Hart Gavin, for her gentle guidance, encouragement, and support. To the special people at Clarkson N. Potter a special "thank you" for their contributions to this book, especially Nancy Novogrod, who came shopping at Cherchez and asked each time if I was ready to do a book.

Deborah Geltman and Gayle Benderoff, for their good sense and unfailing support.

Anne Marie Cloutier for her professionalism and wonderful dedication to the task.

Rochelle Udell and Doug Turshen for their rich creativity and superb problem solving.

Joe Standart and his terrific assistants for their calm and expertise.

Frank Holder, whose exceptional talent in working with flowers lends a special grace to the pages of this book.

Richard Giglio, my favorite artist, whose wonderful flowers bloom on the endpapers of this book.

Everyone at Cherchez, especially Nancy Greene and Camille Prehatney, who kept everything running smoothly and helped with the book, too. Anita Longmire, for the most perfect, impeccable sewing, as usual! Catherine Perret for toting antiques around town. Marnie MacDonald who cared for the children when I was working overtime. Jane Rappeport for all the tips in her wonderful letters from London.

Timothy Mawson, who always found the right volume, and Heidi Friedman of the Horticultural Society of New York.

All the gracious people who shared their beautiful homes, gardens, and treasures with me, Ivan and Alice Bryden, Eileen Collins, Marge Eggleston, Richard and Deborah Geltman, Ed and Anita Holden, Jr., Elizabeth Hubbard, Killearn Farm, Vi Koerner, Joel Mathieson, Lee Ohrbach, Richard Ohrbach, Stewart and Sally Richards, Howard and Doris Roeller, Toni Salvato, Jeri Schwartz, Susan Silver, Joyce Harris Stanton, Tucker and Thorne Taylor, Tony and Susan Victoria, and Randy and Bunny Williams.

The old girl network—Beth Allen, Jean Dimore, Janice Hamilton, Patti McCarthy, Renee Nahas, Lucretia Robertson, Pat Sadowsky, and Norma Sams, my dear friends from corporate days. When I started Cherchez, they planted herbs and tied sachets and now they've helped with this, too.

To Dad, who planted and pruned every night after work in his own garden and still is doing the same in ours. A big thank you for this summer—taking care of children, plants, and stopped-up plumbing, with loving care and expertise —so this book could get finished.

To my wonderful nieces and nephews, Stacey, D.J., Mac, Ricky, Rita, and Harry, and my sister, Linda, for their enthusiasm and interest in all our projects over the years, especially for their involvement with this book and for enriching our lives, always.

My husband, Mel, who really made this book with me and whose encouragement, patience, and kindness have made everything I tackled a joy and a special satisfaction.

CONTENTS

Introduction 1

1

SCENTING
YOUR ROOMS
Potpourri 9

2

Sachets
& Scent Pillows 33

3

Pomanders,
Floral Waters &
Lavender Bottles 45

4

Other Scents 57

5

DECORATING
YOUR HOME
Wreaths 65

6

Bouquets 73

7

Flower
Arrangements 81

8

WORKING
WITH FLOWERS
Growing &
Gathering 89

9

Drying
& Storing 101

10

A Working
Garden 113

SOURCE GUIDE
*Books 120, Gardens 122,
Shops & Supplies 124,
Index 129*

INTRODUCTION

The fragrance of a fresh bouquet of lilacs, of newly cut grass, of freshly laundered linens brings out a special response in all of us. There is something wonderfully evocative about our sense of smell. Of all the five senses, the olfactory is the one most likely to stir up long-forgotten memories. Remember the last time you caught a whiff in the air—the smell of chalk dust, perhaps, or a certain kind of furniture polish—that instantly took you back to a scene in your childhood? The taste of food relies heavily on our sense of smell, and even our moods can be affected by it. Pleasant scents can put you in a wonderful frame of mind. The peace many of us feel when sitting in a garden or park comes not only from the visual surroundings, but also from the comforting smells of nature—flowers, pine needles, moist earth.

Given the key role that it plays in our everyday lives, it's curious that so many of us tend to take this incredible gift for granted. Especially when you stop to consider how easily we can stimulate our sense of smell in ways that give us pleasure and add a new dimension to our personal environment. For me, the easiest and most delightful means of accomplishing this is with flowers. Their reward is twofold. Not only do they look and smell beautiful when first picked, but they can also look and smell just as beautiful when dried. That is what this book is all about—how to incorporate the fragrance as well as the visual beauty of dried flowers into our everyday lives.

I've always been drawn to beautiful things, and my love of flowers is a natural expression of that. My mother and father were both gardening enthusiasts. When we were children, my sister and I helped out with the weeding, and as we got older we became more involved in the planting and picking. My Aunt Jeanette, who has a green thumb, would often show up on weekends with her latest triumph, a seed-

1

Our house is filled all summer with a profusion of flowers from our cutting garden. Picking them is my favorite task.

For me, spring becomes official when the peonies come into bloom and bowls and vases can be filled to overflowing.

The planting season begins with a rediscovery of old clay pots and gardening tools that have become so familiar over the years—like old, trusty friends.

Even though our herb garden is filled with perennials, each spring my husband Mel and I like to add our favorite annuals and try new varieties of plants.

The ingredients for dried potpourri look beautiful even before you mix them, and a glazed crockery bowl is perfect for mixing them in.

Part of Cherchez's collection of antique lingerie, embroidered bed linens, and lacy sachets filled with potpourri.

One of our displays in Cherchez— a table featuring a bountiful bowl of potpourri, room sprays, scented candles, baskets, and fragrant sachets.

A view of our country garden on a midsummer afternoon. At this time of year, there's a profusion of yarrow, pot marjoram, tarragon, and lavender ready for harvest.

ling that was immediately planted by my father in a favorite spot in the garden.

Now, the family gardening tradition continues on in upstate New York, where my husband, Mel, and I have restored an old stone carriage house. Our extended family has always spent the summers together, and we now enjoy working in the gardens surrounded by flowers and young nieces and nephews. Each child loves growing things. And I hope that, like us, they'll continue to do so as they get older.

One thing I remember about my parents' house is that it always seemed to be filled with vases of freshly cut flowers. That, I'd always thought, was the only way flowers could be enjoyed—in a garden or cut and arranged in vases. It wasn't until many years later, when I was working in the fashion industry and covering the couture collections in Europe, that I began to notice what was called *potpourri* —elegant bowls of dried flowers, herbs, spices, and leaves that smelled heavenly. In Europe, potpourri seemed to be everywhere.

My husband and I love to travel. And since he was also in the fashion industry, we spent a lot of time in Europe. We often found ourselves in Venice, which is one of Mel's favorite cities. On one trip we visited the Villa Foscari, a Palladian villa just outside Venice. There, in the center of a huge eight-sided table, was a very large bowl filled with potpourri that intoxicated the air. The sight of it in that spacious, fresco-filled room was so magnificent that we decided to experiment with making our own potpourri.

We are avid collectors of everything, including old herb and flower books.

When we got back home we started to search through them and were excited to discover that we could re-create old potpourri recipes from the sixteenth to the nineteenth century. Some of the ingredients were no longer available, but by modifying the recipes we were still able to create very fragrant and beautiful potpourris.

The results were gratifying, and when Christmas rolled around, we put the potpourri into antique baskets to give as gifts. Everyone who received one was delighted! They loved the fragrance and were intrigued with the idea. It's this same potpourri that still causes people to ask, "What is that wonderful smell?" when they walk into our store, Cherchez.

In fact, you might say that our first experiment with popourri and the adventure of starting our store happened almost simultaneously. It was just about this time that Mel and I became disenchanted with corporate life and its pressures. It seemed that we were always on airplanes going in different directions. So we decided to quit our jobs and bring some order to our hectic lives by starting a business we could work at together.

That first shop of ours was stocked almost exclusively with antique treasures that we'd collected on our European travels: boxes, tea caddies, frames of sterling silver and tortoiseshell, hand-painted china dishes, tureens and teapots, cut-glass decanters, papier-mâché, and a wondrous assortment of antique textiles —Chinese robes garnished with silk embroidery, lacy batiste lingerie and bed linens from Victorian trousseaus. We also decided to sell our potpourri, which seemed to fit in with, and be a natural

extension of, the antiques in our shop.

Happily, our new business was a success. Now, ten years later, we have a larger shop and have opened a second. We sell our line of fragrances for the home—which includes not only our original potpourri but many other things like room sprays, candles, and drawer liners—to other stores here and in Europe. From the very beginning, Cherchez has reflected a personal belief that we should all live and furnish our homes with objects that are well made and beautiful, things lovingly crafted by hand many years ago or by skilled artisans today. And I have always felt that one's home should smell as beautiful as it looks. Why shouldn't we dry or "recycle" the beauty that is growing around us outside into lovely fragrant things for use indoors? Not long ago, I came across an article by Anatole Broyard in which he describes old objects as being "twice touched, rubbed with relevance, tattered or dog-eared with use, corroded with sentiment, caressed by time." Twice touched. I love that phrase. And I think it's an idea that appeals to the collector in all of us.

In one sense, the flowers in this book have been twice touched, too: appreciated once as they grew in the garden, then treasured again in their dried state as decorative elements in the home. In today's world I find it not just nice but necessary to surround myself and my family with things that are familiar, warm, reassuring. Bountiful bowls of pomanders, graceful dried wreaths and bouquets, even sweetly scented sachets can add a measure of civility and pleasure to our lives. To me, it's like leaving little presents all around the house.

The first and second parts of this book are filled with many ideas for scenting and decorating your home with dried flowers. Then, in the third part, I've included some important information about selecting, growing, drying, and storing the botanicals you'll need for these projects. You can either grow your own flowers and herbs for drying or order your botanicals already dried. Generally, the botanical suppliers list the items in their catalogues by their common names, not their Latin ones, so I've done the same throughout the book.

The last chapter is the story of a working garden—my garden, in fact. Even if the most you can manage in the way of gardening is a pot of herbs on a sunny windowsill, I hope it will inspire you to enjoy the beautiful flowers available to us everywhere.

Finally, there is a guide in the back that includes a list of special sources for just about everything you'll need. I've also added a list of books that I hope will help to expand your interest in flowers and fragrance.

One final thought before you turn the page. Working with flowers is fun and you should enjoy doing it. Don't be afraid to use your imagination. The recipes I've given are only a guide. Experiment with your essential oils; each person's sense of smell is individual. Substitute your favorite flowers in a floral bouquet—I love peonies, but you may not. The addition of flowers and the introduction of fragrance to your home should be a personal statement. Perhaps, in some small but special way, this book will open new doors, stimulate new ideas—and you will create your own "scented rooms."

Barbara Milo Ohrbach
New York City
Fall 1985

Scenting Your Rooms

1

POTPOURRI

Potpourri. For me, the word conjures up a room in a comfortable old country house that has mellowed with time. Sun slants through large french doors opening onto a garden. Scattered throughout the room are chintz-covered easy chairs and polished wood tables topped with old photographs, mementos, books. There is a beautiful scent in the air—roses, lavender, a hint of tuberose. It's coming not from the garden, as you might expect, but from a big antique china bowl on one of the tables. The bowl is filled to the brim with fragrant potpourri—flowers, herbs, and spices, all scented with rich oils.

The art of making potpourri is an ancient one, older than the pharaohs. In the Middle Ages, it was diligently practiced by housewives in their stillrooms. In the Victorian era, it was as established a feature as afternoon tea and calling cards. Even today, in the great historic houses of Europe and America, it's not

uncommon to find a beautiful bowl of potpourri—made from a recipe that may go back for generations—welcoming visitors with its heavenly scent.

Given this long tradition, it's no wonder that the making of potpourri strikes so many people as some dark, mysterious process that's quite beyond their abilities. Yet there's really no mystery involved in making potpourri. It's as easy as following a cooking recipe.

But let's start at the beginning. What is potpourri? Basically, it's a mixture of dried flowers and other ingredients placed in a decorative container to add fragrance to the air of a room. A true potpourri smells absolutely wonderful and can keep its scent for a very long time.

There are many prepared potpourris available on the market, but they're not always of the best quality. You may take one home and find that it has no scent at all, or that the scent it does have quickly fades. Or worse, it may not smell very

9

Far left: *Ingredients for making dry potpourri set among antique bowls and jars, an apothecary, mortar and pestle.* Left: *The dried flowers shown here include* (top to bottom): *marigolds, blue malva, roses, lavender, roman chamomile, and hibiscus.*

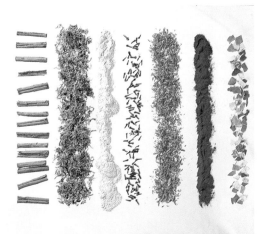

A potpourri might also include such dried botanicals as (left to right): *cinnamon sticks, cut oakmoss, powdered orrisroot, whole cloves, cedar shavings, ground nutmeg, and cut orange peel.*

Some dried potpourri ingredients. Top row, left to right: *whole nutmeg, quassia chips, and patchouli leaves.* Middle row: *Uva ursi, lemon verbena leaves, and lemongrass.* Bottom row: *chamomile flowers, broken cinnamon sticks, and safflower.*

nice to begin with—which defeats the purpose of having potpourri in your home in the first place.

One way to make sure you're getting good potpourri is to buy the very best quality when you can. Another way is to make the potpourri yourself. And that's what I'll be talking about here—how to make a fine, fragrant potpourri that you can enjoy living with (and looking at) for many years to come.

In order to achieve that end, all the ingredients used in your potpourri must be of the highest quality, and I can't emphasize that too strongly. Otherwise you'll end up with a mixture that doesn't smell as it should. It's like a cooking recipe; inferior ingredients will produce an inferior result. So if you're going to go through the trouble of preparing it, investing your time and effort, you'd be wise to work with the best ingredients you can find. As for the ingredients themselves, there are four basic elements in a potpourri: flowers and leaves, herbs and spices, fixatives, and essential oils.

Flowers and Leaves. Dried flower heads or flower petals are the first requirement. You can start with flowers and leaves—from your own garden or a generous friend's—or check out botanical suppliers like the ones listed in the source guide in back of the book, or simply go to a flower shop. Very often, your local florist has flowers that haven't sold and are already in full bloom and ready to be discarded. If you tell the owner that you're making potpourri, he may be willing to give them to you. I've gotten all kinds of wonderful flowers this way because a florist feels that at least those past-their-prime blooms won't be wasted. See Chapter 8 for flowers that are especially suitable for drying to use in potpourris—either mixed in or just placed on top for visual effect.

Herbs and Spices. Since many flowers lose their fragrance after they've been wholly or partially dried, herbs and spices are used to add scent to the potpourri. They include the roots, berries, seeds, or fruits of a variety of aromatic plants like cinnamon, nutmeg, mace, rosemary, and many others. These can be ordered from apothecaries and botanical suppliers, and some can be found easily in your supermarket.

Fixative. Just as the name implies, it's an element used to fix or stabilize the scent of your potpourri. After you've blended all the ingredients together, the fixative—whether in liquid form, powder, or pounded into pieces—is what makes the scent continue to smell. In the old recipes, musk (from deer), civet (from the civet cat), and ambergris (from the sperm whale) were widely used as fixatives. Nowadays, in the interests of ecology, economy, and practicality, those sources are no longer available. As substitutes we have many different kinds of fixatives including benzoin, orrisroot, vetiver, oakmoss (an old favorite in Edwardian potpourris), and storax. Most of these fixatives can be found at apothecaries or botanical suppliers.

I find that powdered orrisroot, which is derived from the florentine iris and smells faintly of violets, is the fixative most readily available from botanical supply sources and one that easily takes on the scent of whatever else you add to it. There is one drawback, however: in its powdered form, orrisroot can make your potpourri look dusty if you use too much.

Essential Oil. Last on the list (and usually in a recipe) but by no means the least important element, essential oil is the

pure, unadulterated oil of a flower, spice, or herb. It's what you add to give the potpourri its desired scent. You might use a single oil essence, like lavender, or combine several—as they do when making perfume—to create whatever fragrance you like. The flowers, spices, herbs, and fixatives may all contribute to the blend, but the essential oil is what dominates it.

Earlier I mentioned the importance of using the best-quality ingredients. This holds especially true when you're selecting an essential oil. There are recipes that advise using an eau de cologne instead of essential oil, but I don't recommend it. Eau de cologne contains alcohol, which causes the scent to evaporate quickly when it's exposed to air. Essential oil, on the other hand, is pure, and because it is, will help the potpourri to keep its fragrance for a longer period of time.

Essential oils are often available in two forms, natural and synthetic, and both may vary in quality and strength. Which form to choose? That depends. Attar of roses, for example, is one of the natural oils that many people associate with potpourri—and with good reason. It's an essence that was used from the very beginning of the potpourri tradition, mainly because certain roses (like the lovely damask rose) tend to keep their fragrance even after they've been wholly or partially dried. But attar of roses is so costly to produce that if you tried to buy it in its natural form, it would cost upward of several thousand dollars a pound.

There are some natural oils that are within a realistic price range. And when you can get it, go with the natural form. But that doesn't mean that the synthetic form is inferior. Many synthetic oils smell beautiful. To make sure they do, always buy the best quality.

When our shop, Cherchez, first started, my husband and I culled recipes from old herb and flower books, adapting and updating them to make our own potpourris from scratch. We grew and bought all the raw ingredients, everything from flowers to expensive essential oils, and blended all the elements that we loved to smell. We kept this up for a year or so until business became so brisk that it was no longer possible to find time to mix it all ourselves. So we gathered up our potpourris and brought them to a fine perfumer who analyzed the recipes we had blended and then created oils that smelled exactly like them. These essential oils of ours are expensive to make, but we felt strongly about using them, and still do. To buy essential oils, check the source guide at the back of the book.

There are two ways of making potpourri, the dry method and the moist. The dry method is the easier and quicker of the two, and therefore the one I would recommend trying—especially if this is the first time you've ever made potpourri. The moist method, though more involved and time-consuming, is the oldest way of making potpourri, and for those of you who would like to try your hand at it, I've included a recipe and directions for this method as well.

DRY POTPOURRI

You can create some very beautiful potpourris using this method. By periodically replenishing it with essential oils, you can keep a bowl of potpourri smelling strongly all through the year.

The first rule for making dry potpourri is that the flowers, herbs, spices, and leaves—in short, all the ingredients except for the essential oil—must be bone-dry. Petals, for instance, should have the crispness of cornflakes. The reason is that even a trace of dampness in any of the original ingredients can cause the potpourri to mildew and leave you with a sorry mess. This is especially important to keep in mind when drying the

Lavender, cloves, allspice, and cinnamon are some of the ingredients for Spicy Lavender Potpourri.

Spicy Lavender Potpourri, left, is shown with a collection of South Staffordshire bowls, pitchers, and dishes.

ingredients yourself (as described in Chapters 8 and 9).

Even if you grow your own, you will still have to buy some ingredients, for example, patchouli leaves, quassia chips, and lemongrass, which may not grow in this country or be readily available. Most botanicals are available already dried from the botanical suppliers noted in the source guide at the back of the book.

The second rule is that a dry potpourri should look as beautiful as it smells. When you consider the fragrance of the ingredients that will go into your blend, you should also be thinking about colors, shapes, and textures. For example, in the Old English Rose recipe that follows, I decided to add some roman chamomile even though it wasn't in the original eighteenth-century version. I liked the look of the white flowers against the reds and pinks of the other petals. Roman chamomile happens to be one of the few white flowers that keeps its color and doesn't dry brown, so its whiteness makes the other colors seem more vivid by contrast. Also, the texture and shape of these petals act as a nice counterpoint to the curled, distinctive shape of the roses.

If you're feeling especially creative, you can add pieces of bark, seeds of certain dried flowers, and roots of others—anything that might add interest to the colors, textures, and shapes in the blend as a whole. Sometimes I like to "finish" the look of my potpourris with the addition of whole dried flower heads that echo the dominant colors of the mix, and I've made suggestions for these at the end of each dry potpourri recipe.

Before you start, you'll need to assemble the following, most of which will be found in any well-furnished kitchen:

A kitchen scale that indicates ounce measures (or a postal scale). While some old recipes call for cupfuls of this and handfuls of that, there is such a thing as being too casual. And if you're making a recipe for the first time, it's always best to stick to specific measures, which in the recipes that follow are converted to ounces.

A mortar and pestle like the kind you'd use to crush kitchen herbs. There are some recipes which require crushed or powdered ingredients, and that's when you'll need the mortar and pestle. I have one in wood and one in stone, and while either will do, I prefer the stone one because it doesn't absorb oils, making it perfect for potpourri preparation.

Several wooden spoons for mixing. These should be bought new and used only for potpourri. Spoons that you've already used for cooking will have traces of food scents on them that could interfere with the floral scents of the potpourri. Conversely, if you use your potpourri spoons for cooking afterward, your soups could end up smelling like roses!

One or more glass or glazed pottery mixing bowls in which you'll mix your recipe. Plastic or wooden bowls won't do because they tend to retain odors from past use and will absorb the essential oils added to the potpourri as you mix.

A scoop for scooping ingredients out of the bags, boxes, or baskets in which they're stored.

A glass eyedropper for adding the essential oil. If you're using more than one oil, be sure to wash the eyedropper out thoroughly between uses so the scent of one doesn't mix with another. Or you may want to buy several inexpensive plastic eyedroppers at the drugstore, then label each one with the name of the essential oil it's used for. It saves the trouble of washing up.

Here are the five recipes I've chosen and adapted from old ones. Each has a distinct charm of its own—both visually and fragrantly—and each will yield about 16 ounces of potpourri or enough to fill a medium-sized bowl. If you'd like to make more than the recipe calls for, to

give as gifts or to make sachets, simply multiply the recipe.

All leftovers should be stored in airtight glass jars (tinted Ball jars are ideal for this) and put in a cool, dry, dark place like a closet to prevent the color and scent from fading before you're ready to use it.

Making Dry Potpourri

The ingredients in these recipes are all listed in order of mixing and should be followed accordingly. There's a good reason for this, and it goes back to what I was saying about the visual appeal of a good potpourri. Certain ingredients are more delicate than others, and because of that, they are added later to avoid their being crushed by heavier ones.

1. Gently mix all the flowers and dry ingredients together in a large glass or glazed pottery bowl.

2. With an eyedropper, scatter the drops of the essential oil all over the combined mixture of flowers and dry ingredients and stir. All of your stirring motions should be extremely gentle in order to avoid crushing the more delicate ingredients.

3. Place the mixture in a roomy brown paper bag that you've lined with wax paper (so the oils won't seep through). Fold and seal the top of the paper bag with a paper clip or clothespin and put in a dry, dark, cool place to "cure" for about two weeks.

4. Every two days or so, turn the contents gently with a wooden spoon to disperse and blend the ingredients so that the scents of the herbs, spices, and oils will permeate one another.

5. After it's cured, the potpourri is ready to be placed in a decorative container. Fill the bowl to the brim so that a mound forms in the middle to give the potpourri some dimension.

SPICY LAVENDER POTPOURRI

I adore lavender because it's such a crisp, evocative scent. This potpourri, with its predominantly purple-and-brown color scheme, looks as lovely as it smells. There's a festiveness about Spicy Lavender that makes it a perfect potpourri to have around the house during the winter holidays.

Incidentally, if you've ever considered growing your own flowers to dry for potpourri, lavender plants would be a good place to start. I've found them to be hardy and I especially like the Hidcote variety that my husband and I grow in our country garden.

> *5 ounces lavender flowers*
> *2 ounces blue malva flowers*
> *1 ounce cornflowers*
> *3 ounces whole cloves*
> *1 ounce crushed cloves*
> *1 ounce cinnamon sticks, broken into*
> *   1-inch pieces*
> *1 ounce cassia chips*
> *½ ounce powdered allspice*
> *½ ounce powdered cinnamon*
> *1 ounce powdered orrisroot*
> *15 drops lavender oil*

To top off your Spicy Lavender Potpourri, you might want to add whole dried heads of purple or lavender irises.

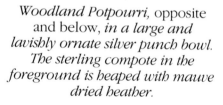

Above and below: *Cherchez's Old English Rose Potpourri in an old-fashioned setting of family photos and glass decanters. The white flowers in the glass compote are roman chamomile.*

Woodland Potpourri, opposite and below, *in a large and lavishly ornate silver punch bowl. The sterling compote in the foreground is heaped with mauve dried heather.*

CHERCHEZ'S OLD ENGLISH ROSE POTPOURRI

If you've ever visited any of the famous gardens in England—Sissinghurst in Kent is my personal favorite—you'll have seen why the English rose has earned such a wide reputation. The rose gardens there are so glorious and lush, and the roses themselves so large, that other gardens seem almost miniature by comparison. A lot of the old shrub roses are grown there, and the resulting fragrance is overwhelmingly beautiful. It's exactly the kind of scent you'll discover in this potpourri which we adapted from an eighteenth-century recipe. It represents what most people refer to when they speak of a classic potpourri.

Old English Rose is also the first potpourri recipe we developed to sell at Cherchez. Even now, people who say that they never liked the scent of roses ("too sweet" or "too cloying for my taste") fall in love with this potpourri whenever they smell it. It's more of a misty rose scent, dusky rather than sweet, which is really what a rose garden smells like.

Visually, the medley of deep red, pink, and white is very appealing and looks beautiful in most any setting.

5 ounces pink rose petals
2 ounces red rose petals
2 ounces roman chamomile flowers
1 ounce heather flowers
2 ounces quassia chips
2 ounces lemongrass
1 ounce powdered orrisroot
1 ounce oakmoss, cut into 1-inch
  pieces
20 drops rose, tea rose, or rose
  geranium oil

If you like, you can add whole rose heads, in red and pink, on top of the potpourri after placing it in a pretty bowl.

WOODLAND POTPOURRI

Patchouli, the predominant scent in the Woodland blend, is another of my favorites. It always makes me think of forests and old tailored tweeds—which is why I think it's such a great potpourri for a man's apartment or a library. But this distinctive yet subtle scent would work in any environment.

The colors are mostly dark with lots of deep reds and browns. I've added rosebuds for texture. There is a good amount of powder in this recipe, so if you plan to display it in a glass bowl, be careful when filling it to avoid dusting up the glass.

3 ounces pink rosebuds
4 ounces patchouli leaves
2 ounces hibiscus petals
2 ounces dark-red rose petals
2 ounces cedar shavings
1 ounce powdered orrisroot
8 drops patchouli oil
2 ounces peony petals

Note: In order to keep the peony petals nice and whole, I suggest mixing all the other dry ingredients first, then adding the oil, and finally the peonies.

A nice finishing touch: whole dried peony heads in deep, deep red.

COTTAGE GARDEN POTPOURRI

This is what you might call the stockpot of potpourris because even after it's made you can keep replenishing the variegated blend with any dried flowers you happen to have on hand. The centerpiece from your last dinner party, the bouquet of roses you got for your birthday, the first spring flowers that shoot up in the garden—all can be dried and added to a Cottage Garden Potpourri. As for the scent, you can add any floral essential oil that pleases you.

For the recipe below, I've chosen flowers that are easily obtainable, either locally or from a botanical supplier. If more exotic varieties come your way, don't hesitate to add them to the potpourri as you like.

2 ounces pink rosebuds
1 ounce lavender flowers
1 ounce chamomile flowers
2 ounces cornflowers
2 ounces uva ursi leaves, or any
  dried, dark-green leaves
2 ounces hibiscus petals
1 ounce peony petals
3 ounces marigold flowers
1 ounce blue malva flowers
1 ounce powdered orrisroot
20 drops of any one floral essential oil
  you prefer, such as rose geranium,
  jasmine, lily of the valley,
  honeysuckle, or heliotrope

Note: Since peony, marigold, and malva flowers tend to be more fragile than the others, mix them in last, after you add the essential oil.

While nearly any whole, dried flower heads will complement the Cottage Garden Potpourri, I particularly like adding whole, bright-yellow daffodils.

CITRUS POTPOURRI

There are some wonderful textures to be found in this potpourri, as well as a nice variety of shapes. The color palette is primarily oranges with yellows and a dash of green. The scent is bright, tangy, and fresh as an orange grove—not a pure orange, but something more tempered and sophisticated.

You can buy dried orange peel from a botanical supplier, but why not recycle the peels from the oranges you eat at home? Just peel the orange, then cut or tear the peel into inch-sized pieces. To dry, place the pieces on a cookie sheet and leave out for a few days. When the peels have hardened, they're ready to use in your potpourri.

You could do this with lemon and lime peels as well, and even if you don't use them in a potpourri recipe, it's a marvelous way to scent your kitchen. Just place all the peels in a pretty bowl and add one of the citrus essential oils.

4 ounces cut orange peel
4 ounces marigold flowers
3 ounces chamomile flowers
1 ounce cut lemongrass
1 ounce powdered orrisroot
20 drops lemon or lemon verbena oil
3 ounces lemon verbena leaves

Note: Since lemon verbena leaves are very brittle and delicate, add them last, after you've mixed your other ingredients and added the oil. Then stir them extremely gently into the mixture.

A colorful addition to the Citrus Potpourri would be dried daffodils or orange tiger lilies.

Cottage Garden Potpourri, above and below, *topped with bright yellow daffodil heads. Echoing the brass bowl are antique English brass candlesticks next to a wooden pear-shaped tea caddy.*

Citrus Potpourri, below and opposite, *topped with lilies. The French and Scandinavian country earthenware pieces reflect the colors of the potpourri.*

Containers for Potpourri

There are any number of wonderful containers you could use for potpourri. I almost have more fun choosing them than I do making the potpourri itself, because it gives me an excuse for visiting every antiques shop, antiques show, and craft market that I can.

The container should be just as pretty as the mixture it holds, and you should keep that in mind when making your selection. A sparkling glass bowl, for example, is perfect for showing off the colors and textures of the ingredients, but porcelain, pottery, and baskets will all work equally well (line a basket with foil first so the potpourri doesn't seep through). I also like the idea of using a sterling silver bowl—either very simple or very ornate—for holding potpourri. The same goes for any metal like brass or copper that's been buffed to a mirror shine. I find that the counterpoint of polished metal against the natural, textured elements of the potpourri can be especially pleasing. Hand-painted porcelain or pottery bowls make wonderful potpourri containers (early nineteenth-century Continental, English, or American versions are especially pretty and delicate looking).

Whatever your choice of container, see that it's compatible with the colors and period of the room in which it's going to be placed. When in doubt, it's always better to go with the simplest designs rather than with something more ornate that may be questionable.

Along with choosing the perfect container for the dry potpourri you've made, you also have to decide where you're going to place it. Potpourris are especially effective in small rooms, like a study, foyer, dressing room, or bedroom. If the room is so large that the bouquet of the mixture gets lost, you might want to place the potpourri bowl so that it scents a specific area—for example, in the corner of a living room or study near an easy chair, or on a dressing table. Potpourri on a night table is wonderful, too—you can fall asleep with (and wake up to) its glorious fragrance every day. Potpourris also work well in any room that's open to gentle breezes. The draft then carries and disperses the scent.

Don't put potpourri in direct sunlight because the sun will fade the color of the flowers. If you like the idea of adding fragrance to your closets and drawers, use sachets which are made for that purpose (see the next chapter).

Refreshing Dry Potpourri

One of the nicest things about potpourri is that you never need to throw it away. If the colors of the flowers fade, either from age or from direct exposure to sunlight, you can simply add freshly dried flowers to the blend and stir.

But when most people ask about refreshing a potpourri, they're referring to the scent, and when the scent fades it can be for a variety of reasons. For one thing, there's the time element to consider. Though essential oils are extremely long-lasting, they will gradually weaken over a period of months. A potpourri can lose its scent from having been exposed to air —and this is to be expected.

Many people come into our shop absolutely crestfallen because the potpourri they've made has lost its scent. They blame themselves for doing something wrong. What I advise them to do is simply refresh the potpourri with the same essential oil that was used in its making. If you're not sure what essential oil was used—because, say, the potpourri was given to you as a gift—or if the remaining scent is very weak, you can use any essential oil you prefer.

How much oil is enough? That depends. The strength of a fragrance is a matter of individual choice. However, it's always a good idea to start with less. Think of it in the same terms as adding salt in cooking; you can always add more later, but you can't take it out if you've added too much. Your best bet is to add several drops of essential oil, mix it into the potpourri, then live with it for a few days. If it still isn't strong enough after that time, you can add more oil.

Another trick is to stir the potpourri gently; the resulting small breakage of the chips, twigs, and petals will help the scent to regenerate. (Lavender, for example, will always give off a stronger scent when you crush the flowers in your hand.)

I know that some people like to refresh their potpourri with a few drops of brandy, but I've never tried this myself. The refreshening process is more effective when you stay with the same scent rather than introducing a new one, and essential oils are the way to achieve this.

Some people like to cover their bowls of potpourri when they're not at home or when they don't have guests. It's true that the less you expose the mixture to air, the longer it will last. But I don't believe in saving the beauty of potpourri for special occasions. I enjoy being welcomed by it when I come home from my day and living with it all the time. And so should you.

MOIST POTPOURRI

One of my favorite garden designers is Gertrude Jekyll. Her books on gardening are a treasure and when she talks about potpourri in *Home and Garden,* published in England in 1900, she says: "The dry is much the easier and quicker to make, but is neither so sweet nor so enduring, so now the moist is the only kind I care to have."

And Miss Jekyll is right. The chief advantage to making a moist potpourri is that the ingredients, being partially dried, retain most of their beautifully scented natural oils. This produces a blend that's much longer-lasting and stronger-smelling than dry potpourri—one that rarely, if ever, needs to be refreshed.

One drawback which Miss Jekyll also mentions is the time and attention required to make a moist potpourri. Try it if you have lots of patience and enjoy long projects, because it can take anywhere from two weeks to an entire summer to finish.

Another consideration is that, although it smells wonderful, a finished moist potpourri isn't particularly attractive to look at. It must be placed in a closed container with a lid—one with little holes in the top so the scent can escape into the room.

The moist method is the oldest way of making potpourri, but there are so many different versions that people often tend to be confused. Actually, there are just two basic steps. The first is mixing partially dried flower petals with salt and allowing the mixture to ferment. The second is adding spices and herbs and letting the potpourri·mellow or "cure."

Here is a list of the materials you will need and directions for the basic method. Read them through first before you start. Then, I'll be giving you a very special recipe for moist potpourri. Aside from the ingredients themselves, you'll need to assemble the following items for making a moist potpourri:

A *widemouthed, straight-sided container* of nonporous material that's been glazed on the inside and has a cover. A gallon-sized pottery crock would be perfect.

A *long-handled wooden spoon* for mixing the ingredients.

A *heavy dish or saucer* that's slightly smaller than the circumference of the container.

*Bowls of dried potpourri look beautiful anywhere—
whether the setting is airy and romantic like the
lace-and-chintz bedroom,* opposite, *or cozy and
traditional like the library,* above, *with its paisley chair,
tartan throw, and shelves of books.*

An iron doorstop or heavy rock that fits inside the container. You'll be placing this on top of the dish or saucer to fashion a weight for pressing the petals and salt down into the crock.

Coarse, noniodized salt (no matter what kind of salt a moist potpourri recipe may suggest using, kosher or sea salt will work just as well, as long as it's coarse and noniodized. Both are available in most supermarkets).

Two mixing bowls with glazed interiors.

Making Moist Potpourri

Drying
1. Partially dry the rose or other flower petals needed for the recipe. (Be sure to use flowers that are fresh from the garden, or if bought at the florist's, make sure the petals are very fragrant.) The petals should be placed in a single layer on a window screen or newspaper and set in a dark, airy place such as a closet or under a bed.
2. When the petals become limp and have a soft, leathery texture, they are sufficiently dry. This may take up to three or four days, so check each day. If the petals become too dry, or totally dry, you won't be able to use them in a moist potpourri, but you can save them to use in a dry one.

Layering Petals and Salt
3. Place a layer of petals in the crock and sprinkle them with a layer of salt (a ratio of three to one, petals to salt). This will absorb excess moisture from the partially dried petals. Continue layering in that order until the crock is almost full. This can be done all at one time or over several weeks as you collect more petals.
4. Place the heavy weight on the dish and use this to push the petal/salt layers down

into the crock, pressing down hard. Leave the weight in place so that each day you can press down in order to make the mixture cake together. Cover and store the crock on an accessible shelf in a dry place.
5. Each day, before pressing the mixture, remove the dish and weight so you can stir it. Using a wooden spoon, scrape any residue from the sides of the crock, then turn the contents with a folding movement as if you were folding egg whites into a soufflé. If a froth appears, don't worry. Just mix it in with the petals. If liquid accumulates in the bottom of the crock, drain it off. (Use this fragrant residue to scent dry potpourri.)
6. Continue the daily stirring/pressing procedure until a dense caking of all the ingredients occurs. Then you're ready for the next stage.

Mixing Herbs and Spices
7. Empty the caked mass from the crock into one of the mixing bowls and crumble it with your hands.
8. In the other mixing bowl, blend whatever herbs and spices are called for in the recipe. This may be done hours, or even days, ahead. Just keep the mixture in a closed container until you need it.
9. Combine the crumbled petal mixture with the herb/spice mixture in one bowl and blend with the wooden spoon.

Aging
10. Initially, the potpourri may smell very "new" or "raw" to you, but the aging process is intended to correct this. Return the ingredients to their crock and press them down with the dish/weight until they're tightly packed.
11. Cover the crock with a piece of muslin and secure with a rubber band.
12. Place the muslin-covered crock back in the closet for six weeks in order to age or mellow the potpourri. *Note:* If you want to add essential oil, which is optional, do it at this point. A few drops will do.

LADY BETTY GERMAIN'S RECIPE

The English have a very special way with flowers and gardens. They are inspired and practical at the same time, and the results are often glorious. Sissinghurst Castle Gardens was planted by Vita Sackville-West and her husband, Harold Nicolson. She is primarily known for her wonderful books on gardening, but she wrote many others including one on Knole, her ancestral birthplace—which is where I discovered Lady Betty Germain and her marvelous recipe for moist potpourri.

Knole is one of the grandest of England's stately homes. Its collection of antique tapestries and rare fabrics is extensive—in fact, it has its own textile conservation department set up within the house itself. It was this attraction that made a visit to Knole a must for my husband and me.

Although it was a cold day in November, we were cheered considerably at the sight of the delightful lady who was to act as our National Trust guide. She graciously led us through the different rooms, each one more beautiful than the last. Finally, we came to the most extraordinary rooms of all, a small suite adorned with rich eighteenth-century needlework. Flowers were hand-embroidered on chairs and bed coverings and woven into wall hangings. And on a table, filling the rooms with its lovely fragrance, was a bowl of potpourri. When I asked about it, I was told that the potpourri was made every summer at Knole using a recipe of Lady Betty Germain's—whose rooms these had once been. The mixture was still being made almost as she had made it in 1750.

The recipe that follows is my adaptation of the original formula. I've added quantities where none were given and substituted similar botanicals and oils for those that are no longer available or difficult to find. (The art of potpourri was not a science in 1750, so you can approximate your ingredients.) This should make about one gallon of moist potpourri.

Layer the following ingredients as described in steps 1 through 6 for making moist potpourri:

> *approximately 3–3½ pounds flower petals, which can include:*
> *rose petals*
> *violets*
> *lavender flowers*
> *lemon verbena leaves*
> *rosemary*
> *lemon balm*
> *rose geranium leaves*
> *1 pound coarse, noniodized salt*

For the spice mixture, blend the following ingredients as described in steps 7 through 9:

> *½ ounce powdered cinnamon*
> *½ ounce powdered mace*
> *½ ounce powdered nutmeg*
> *½ ounce cut lemon peel*
> *2 ounces powdered orrisroot*
> *1 ounce powdered gum benzoin*
> *several drops rose or rose geranium essential oil (optional)*

To finish, follow steps 10 through 12.

Remember that a moist potpourri smells much prettier than it looks, so if you want to put it in an open bowl, I'd suggest you mask the top of it with whole flower heads dried separately in silica gel (see Chapter 9). But if you can find one, the best container for this type of potpourri would be a porcelain or pottery receptacle with a perforated lid. Or you could place your moist potpourri inside a loosely woven, lidded basket lined with aluminum foil.

How long will it last? Some moist potpourris have been said to keep their lovely scent for fifty years—perhaps yours will, too!

Rose petals and salt for moist potpourri

Covered baskets for moist potpourri

Pottery boxes for moist or *dry potpourri*

Right: *A Victorian china jar with
two lids, one perforated, for
holding moist potpourri. In
the bowl are dried rose petals
from the garden.*

2
SACHETS
& SCENT PILLOWS

Sachets have been popular for a long time (Homer even mentions them in the *Odyssey*), which isn't at all surprising, because these small pouches of scent are pretty to look at, and portable, too. You can stash a sachet just about anywhere you'd like to add a touch of fragrance—in closets, drawers, blanket chests, armoires, or desks—tie them onto furniture, or tuck them behind pillows on beds and sofas. In the late eighteenth century, women even wore perfumed sachets in the folds of their billowy long skirts.

They can also be terrific gifts—especially if you've made them yourself. A nice idea is to take a linen handkerchief with lace edging, put several tablespoons of potpourri in the center, bring up the ends, and tie it with pastel silk ribbons, making a very elegant bundle.

Just last year, when one of my dearest friends was in the hospital, I gave her a get-well present with a small sachet tied to the ribbon like a gift card. On a return visit, I saw that she had pinned the sachet to her pillow, and that the nurses and other patients were stopping by to smell and enjoy it as well. I have even been known to carry a sachet in my handbag for emergencies—like riding in stale-smelling taxis. It also makes my handbag smell terrific.

In this chapter, you'll find directions for making seven sachets, each with a different scent and for a different use. If you have any dry potpourri left over from a recipe in the preceding chapter, it can work in a sachet as well. The bags themselves can be run up on a sewing machine in no time.

Selecting Fabrics for a Sachet

While many fabrics will make wonderful-looking sachets, some will work better than others. I prefer fabrics made of natural fibers since they readily allow the scent of the sachet to escape into the air. These include cotton, linen, and silk. Even simple muslin, pillow ticking, or linen toweling can look pretty and fresh with the addition of a colorful ribbon.

Use patterns that are scaled to the size of the bag. Liberty florals, French wallpaper stripes, or small-patterned chintzes are all good choices. Avoid very large prints.

Antique fabric scraps like small quilt pieces or bits of Victorian silk can be made up into truly beautiful sachets. Pieces of handmade lace—old or new—lined with batiste or tulle in solid white or a soft pastel will always look special.

Interesting and pretty ribbons are a must and should be selected to coordinate with your fabrics. In fact, you can even make a sachet from the ribbon itself if it's 1½ inches wide or more.

Opposite: *Sachets in small printed cotton fabrics tucked into a country basket that's been lined with one of the flower prints.*
Above: *Start with a rectangle of fabric; fold, sew, fill it with potpourri, and tie.*

Making a Sachet

Once you've collected your fabrics and ribbons, you're ready to start sewing. To make a very beautiful, nicely finished sachet, do the following:

1. Cut a rectangle of fabric that measures 8 by 11 inches.
2. Fold the fabric in half lengthwise, right sides together, and stitch down the long open side and one short side, using a ½-inch seam allowance.
3. Fold the top of the bag about halfway down over the bag itself and iron. (This piece will stay tucked into the bag when turned right side out.)
4. Turn the bag right side out and fill it two-thirds full with potpourri mixture.
5. Tie it with an 18-inch length of ¼- or ½-inch-wide ribbon, making a double knot and then a bow.

Sachet Recipes

It doesn't matter if the ingredients of a sachet mixture get crushed in the blending because they'll be hidden inside the sachet rather than being on display in a container or jar. Consequently, the directions are simple:

1. Mix all the ingredients in a glazed pottery bowl.
2. Put the potpourri into a brown paper bag lined with wax paper and store in a cool, dark place to age for a period of two weeks. Occasionally stir the contents with a wooden spoon to disperse and blend the oils.
3. When the potpourri has "cured," spoon it into the fabric bags and tie with ribbon.

LAVENDER SACHETS

This is one of my great favorites and also what I consider to be the simplest recipe to make. Since it has few ingredients, it can be quickly made.

It's an especially pleasing scent to find in a lingerie or handkerchief drawer, or in a box of writing paper. I put a sachet in each of my desk drawers and the paper, being an absorbent material, then takes on a light lavender scent.

Lavender flowers are very fragrant (even without the addition of oils), so a nice bonus of this sachet is that it lasts a long time. In little print cotton bags, they'll look as fresh as they smell.

3 ounces lavender flowers
1 ounce powdered orrisroot
4 drops lavender oil

Yield: 4 ounces, or enough to fill four sachets

TRAVEL SACHETS

I dislike hotel rooms that don't smell really fresh—something that can happen in even the best hotels. So whenever I check into a room, be it grand or a *pension,* I put my latest mystery book on the night table and open all the windows. While unpacking, I stash my potent, spicy Travel Sachets into the drawers, tuck some into the closet, and tie one onto the doorknob. Then I close the windows, order tea—and it's just like home.

1 ounce rose petals
½ ounce cinnamon sticks, crushed
½ ounce powdered allspice
½ ounce cut oakmoss
½ ounce rosemary sprigs, crushed
1 ounce whole cloves
1 tonka bean, crushed
2 drops bergamot oil

Yield: 4 ounces, or enough to fill four sachets

LEMON FURNITURE SACHETS

There's nothing like a good English lemon wax for polishing fine wood furniture. It even smells shiny—and that's why I love the idea of Lemon Furniture Sachets. You can tie them onto bedposts or chair backs or tuck them behind a shelf of books, and they'll make the room smell freshly polished.

When you make up the bags for this sachet, choose fabrics that coordinate with the colors in your room. Remember to use longer-length ribbons so they can be tied onto chair backs and bedposts easily.

½ ounce lemon verbena leaves
½ ounce lemon balm
½ ounce lemon thyme
½ ounce cut lemon peel
½ ounce chamomile flowers
½ ounce cut oakmoss
4 drops lemon verbena oil

Yield: 3 ounces, or enough to fill four sachets

MOTH SACHETS

One of the main ingredients for this recipe is southernwood, an herb with a longstanding reputation for its ability to repel moths. A literal translation of its name in French, *garde-robe,* describes exactly what these sachets do. They protect your clothes—in fact, your whole winter wardrobe. What's also nice is that they make everything smell wonderful. Southernwood in particular has a haylike scent that seems to bring the outdoors in.

I use Moth Sachets for tucking into blanket chests and sweater drawers and for slipping onto hangers in storage closets. Two sachets per drawer and about four per closet usually do the job.

It's a good idea to make up new

sachets each year so they'll always be potent. By squeezing them every so often, you'll also heighten the scent. And don't throw the old ones away. By rescenting them with a nice essential oil, like rose, you can use them as you would regular sachets.

Since you'll be making a lot of them, the best fabric for Moth Sachets would be something simple like muslin, linen toweling, or pillow ticking.

> 2 ounces southernwood
> 1/2 ounce whole cloves
> 1 ounce cedar shavings
> 1 ounce powdered orrisroot
> 1 ounce cut oakmoss
> 2 cinnamon sticks, crushed

Yield: 6 ounces, or enough to fill seven sachets

MEN'S SHIRT SACHETS

If the smell of stale pipe tobacco and running shoes has taken over your husband's closet, here's a sachet that will help make everything smell fresh and airy again. The bags for it can be made of the pin-striped cotton from one of his old shirts whose cuffs and collars have seen better days. It's a nice way to recycle fabric, and a classic menswear print is the perfect complement for the wonderful outdoorsy scent of the blend itself.

This recipe is an adaptation of the Woodland Potpourri on page 20, but I've eliminated the hibiscus, peony, and rosebuds which were in the potpourri for visual reasons, and I've reduced the quantity of ingredients.

> 1 ounce rose petals
> 1 1/2 ounces patchouli leaves
> 1 ounce cedar shavings
> 1/2 ounce powdered orrisroot
> 2 drops patchouli oil

Yield: 4 ounces, or enough to fill four sachets

BATH BAGS

If you've never come across this particular form of sachet before, you're in for a treat. Several minutes before getting into the tub, swish one of these little bags around in the hot bath water to scent it—and the bathroom—with heavenly fragrance. Afterward, hang the bag from the faucet until the next time. Each sachet is good for several baths.

Since they're going to be plunged into hot water, the best fabric to use for the bag would be unbleached muslin tied with twine instead of ribbon. You can pile the little muslin bags in a basket and place on a shelf or table to have ready for guests and scent the bathroom all at the same time.

> 1 ounce rose petals
> 1 ounce lavender flowers
> 1 ounce rolled oats (for bulk)
> 1/2 ounce cut orange peel
> 1/2 ounce cut lemon peel
> 2 bay leaves, broken
> 2 rosemary sprigs, crushed

Yield: 4 ounces, or enough to fill four sachets

Making a Bath Bag

Follow the directions for making a standard sachet given earlier in this chapter, but with these changes.

1. Cut the fabric to measure 8 by 6 inches.
2. Trim the top of the bag with pinking shears.
3. Use twine instead of ribbon (the bath bag can be hung in the bath from the loops of the bow).

Lace hankie sachets filled with potpourri

Lavender sachets scent a desk drawer

Travel sachets on a hotel room door

Lemon furniture sachet tied onto a chair

Moth sachets for protecting woolens

Men's shirt sachets to freshen dresser drawers

Muslin bath bags in a guest bathroom

Powder sachets made from pretty ribbons

POWDER SACHETS

Sometimes a regular flower and herb mixture is too bulky for its intended use—as it would be for the easy to make ribbon sachet described below. In this case, a powder sachet makes the ideal alternative.

I put these long narrow ribbon sachets filled with scented powder in my linen closet, placing them in the folds of freshly ironed sheets, pillowcases, and tablecloths. When unfolded, the linens emit a lovely scent.

4 ounces cornstarch or unscented talcum
10 drops of your favorite rich, floral essential oil, such as tuberose, magnolia, hyacinth, or jasmine

Yield: 4 ounces, or enough to fill one to two sachets

Making a Powder Sachet

For each one, you'll need 18 inches of pretty decorated ribbon, 1½ to 2 inches wide, and 18 inches of narrow ribbon for tying the top.

1. Fold the wide ribbon in half, right side out. (The finished bag will be 9 inches long.)
2. Stitch the two long sides together as close to the edge as possible.
3. Snip the edges of the open end with pinking shears.
4. Pack the bag tightly with the Powder Sachet mixture.
5. Tie the top of the bag closed with the narrow ribbon, making a double knot and then a bow.

Refreshing a Sachet

The length of time a sachet's fragrance will last depends on where you put it. Sachets placed in a closed drawer or chest will last longer than those tied onto a hanger in a large closet. The more exposed to air the sachet is, the quicker it tends to fade.

When the sachet does fade, you can revive it with a gentle squeeze, which crushes the ingredients to release more of their natural oils.

When more decisive measures are called for, you can refresh the sachet with a few drops of the original essential oil. Just untie the bag and empty the contents into a bowl, mix with the oil, cure for a few days, and return the contents to the bag. With occasional pep-ups, your sachets can last for years.

SCENT PILLOWS

Long before the advent of innerspring mattresses, bedding was stuffed with a variety of aromatic grasses. It's a rather lovely idea (fragrant if not particularly comfortable) that eventually led to the creation of the herb pillow. A pillow filled with herbs and flowers was thought to induce relaxation and sleep and keep bad dreams at bay. No less a personage than George III owned a hop pillow without which he refused to attempt a night's sleep.

As a hopeless insomniac myself, I don't put any store in the sleep-enhancing properties of such pillows. But I do love having scent pillows around the house for tucking under a chaise or bed pillow, or for tossing into my carry-on luggage to use as a neck rest on plane rides. The scent of the fresh herbs and spices, if not a sleeping aid, is definitely relaxing and pleasurable to the senses.

Most of the scent pillows that I've seen are filled with herbs and sewn on all four sides, making it difficult to launder the case or refresh the herbal mixture. Instead, I prefer using a small boudoir or throw pillow filled with down or fiberfill that I cover with a removable sham which has a little outside pocket for holding a sachet. That way, I can remove the bag from the pocket whenever the sham needs to be laundered, and easily refresh the herb mixture in the sachet as often as necessary.

Make a fabric cover for any small pillow you already have, or buy a 12 by 16-inch boudoir pillowcase, and then hand-sew a pocket on the back. If you're having throw pillows made for your sofas and chairs, have the pockets sewn on in the same fabric. Then you can also make co-ordinating sachets from the leftover fabric pieces.

Making the Pocket

1. Cut out a 6-inch square of fabric.
2. Press all four edges under ½ inch.
3. Fold one side under another ¾ inch. Stitch and iron. This will be the top of the pocket.
4. Place the pocket in the center back of the pillowcase or cover.
5. Machine-stitch or hand-sew along the bottom and two sides of the pocket to attach it to the pillowcase.

Making the Sachet

Follow the directions for sewing a sachet on page 35. Use any of the following simple recipes. Each incorporates several herbs that are said to induce relaxation and sleep. To make, mix the dried ingredients and essential oil in a glazed pottery bowl. Put the mixture in a brown bag lined with wax paper, and store in a cool place for two weeks. Occasionally stir the contents with a wooden spoon to blend the scents.

ROSEMARY SCENT PILLOW

1 ounce lavender flowers
1 ounce sweet woodruff
1 ounce rosemary sprigs
2 drops bergamot oil

Yield: 3 ounces, or enough to fill three sachets

SPICY ROSE SCENT PILLOW

½ ounce peppermint leaves
½ ounce whole cloves
1 ounce rose petals
2 drops rose oil

Yield: 2 ounces, or enough to fill two sachets

LEMON VERBENA SCENT PILLOW

½ ounce peppermint leaves
1 ounce lemon verbena leaves
½ ounce lemon thyme leaves
1 ounce chamomile flowers
2 drops lemon verbena oil

Yield: 3 ounces, or enough to fill three sachets

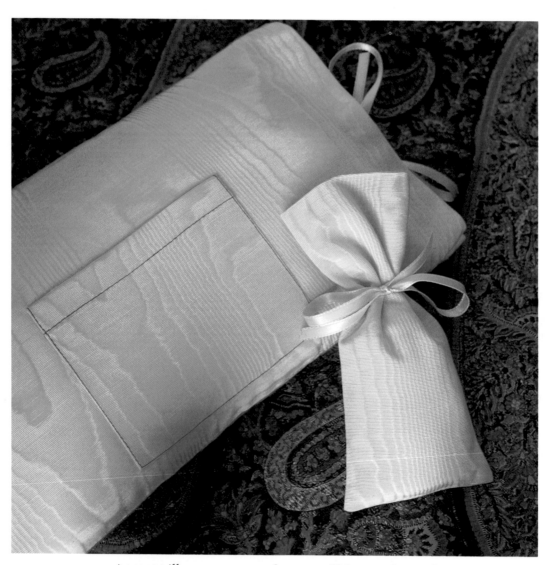

*A scent pillow you can make yourself (we used moiré)
so that the scented sachet fits into the pocket of the
pillowcase. When you're not using it, add it to a
collection of old batiste and lace pillows like
the ones shown,* opposite.

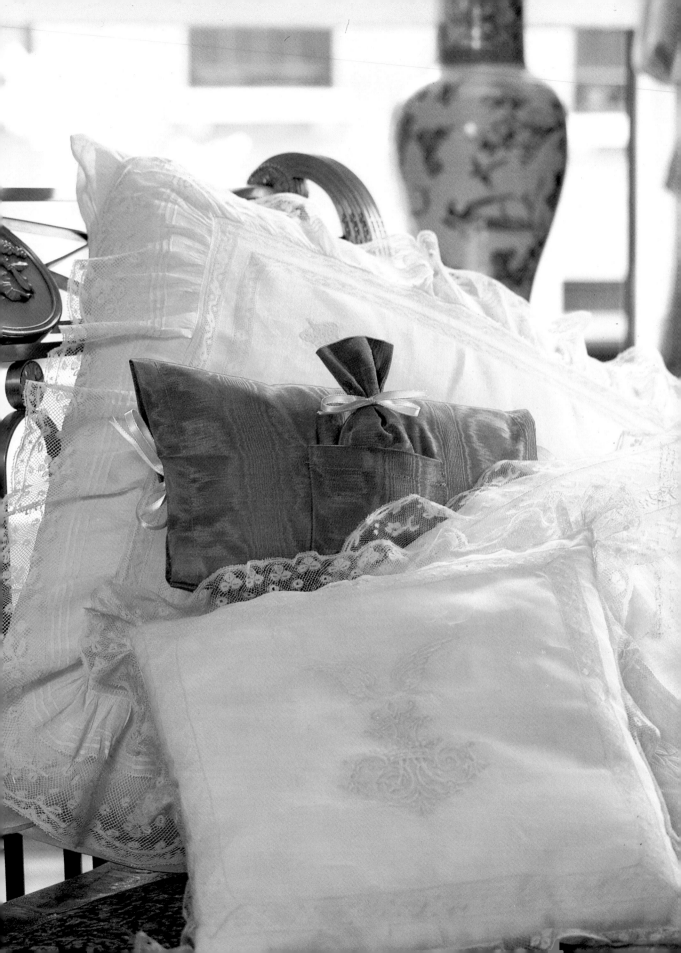

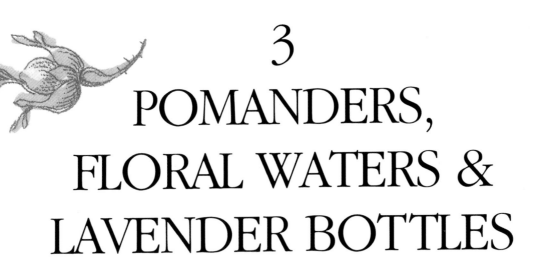

3
POMANDERS,
FLORAL WATERS &
LAVENDER BOTTLES

While potpourri and sachets are some of the most popular and familiar ways of introducing scents into your home, there are also many other lovely ideas that come to mind.

Until the nineteenth century, women had to make almost everything that sat on their dressing tables or in their medicine cupboards. The "still room" was a very important room in the house. That's where the herbs, leaves, spices, barks, berries, roots, grasses, and flowers were gathered after they were dried and made into all the things the household needed in the way of medicine, cosmetics, and scent. They must have been wonderful and mysterious places, filled with strange pungent-smelling botanicals all being

made into something else, equally fragrant and magical.

So, if you've ever wished you were born in an earlier, gentler time, I have a suggestion—try making some pomanders, floral waters, or lavender bottles. These ideas may sound old-fashioned, but it is, in fact, their very old-fashioned quality that makes them so special.

Try filling a large glass compote with pungent pomanders instead of fruit for a change, tucking lavender bottles between the guest towels in your bathroom, or putting floral water in an extra atomizer and spraying it in guests' rooms before they arrive. These things add soothing fragrance, as well as a particular charm to your home.

Opposite: *Ribbon-tied pomanders can be piled into china bowls and enjoyed all year.*
Above: *Finished pomanders cure in a bowl of spice mixture.*

Citrus fruits and apples for pomanders

Making pomanders in our country kitchen

POMANDERS

Originally, a pomander was a small ball of gold, silver, or ivory—often beautifully filigreed—containing pieces of rare-scented spices "fixed" with ambergris. These elegant little spheres, which were hung by a chain from the neck or the waist, were the medieval and Elizabethan solutions for warding off objectionable smells. (Some people even claimed that pomanders had the power to prevent illness.)

Today, pomanders are usually in one of two forms. One is a perforated china ball filled with potpourri. The other, with which we are most familiar, is an orange, an apple, or sometimes a lemon, that's been studded with cloves.

Because they look and smell so festive, pomanders made from fruit have long been a Christmas holiday tradition. But I like having them around the house all year round—mounds and mounds of them piled into bowls all by themselves, or placed on a bed of lavender or rosemary. I also like to tie them with beautiful ribbons and hang them on chandeliers. The wonderful spice-rich aroma is one of the quickest spirit lifters I know. Making pomanders is a perfect project for children, and an ideal way to introduce them to the fun of working with herbs and spices.

In fact, I'm a great believer in getting children involved with flowers and gardening in general. We have six nieces and nephews who share their summers with us in the country, and all of them have been avid gardeners since they were little. They love to help harvest the herbs and flowers for potpourris that we make together, and they're all expert pomander makers, too. The next time your children are cooped up in the house on a rainy day, try sitting them around the kitchen table for a pomander-making project of their own. They'll stay occupied for hours, and your kitchen will smell glorious.

Making a Pomander

You will need the following to make a pomander:

Firm, thin-skinned oranges or apples. These should be free of blemishes. Lemons or limes would also be suitable.

Whole, large-headed cloves. Buy top quality for visual effect and make sure they have a good, strong smell.

Curing spice mixture (see recipe below).

A thin, metal crochet hook or knitting needle. For piercing the fruit. This makes the job quicker and easier on the fingers.

Large glazed pottery bowl in which you'll cure the pomanders.

Small bowl for mixing spices.

1. As you insert the cloves, hold the fruit firmly but don't squeeze it. The cloves can be placed into the fruit at random or in a linear pattern, which is much neater looking. Be sure the cloves are close together but not crowding one another. They should be far enough apart so as to prevent splitting the skin of the fruit. A thin, metal crochet hook or knitting needle can be used for piercing the fruit wherever you insert a clove. If you want to hang your pomander from a ribbon, leave a ½-inch "path" around the fruit. This will act as a groove to hold the ribbon in place. (It also cuts down on clove-studding time.)

The insertion of cloves should be finished on the same day as it's begun. If you leave the pomander unfinished overnight, the unstudded part of the fruit may begin to rot.

2. Blend the curing spice mixture in the small bowl.

3. Sprinkle about half of this mixture into the bottom of the large bowl and place the studded pomanders on top.

4. Sprinkle the rest of the spice mixture over the pomanders.

5. Each day, turn the pomanders and sprinkle them with the spice mixture.

Continue this process daily until the pomanders are totally hardened. This may take anywhere from two weeks to over a month, depending on the size of the fruit. When the pomanders have hardened, they are ready.

CURING SPICE MIXTURE

4 ounces powdered cinnamon
2 ounces powdered cloves
½ ounce powdered allspice
½ ounce powdered nutmeg
1 ounce powdered orrisroot

Yield: 8 ounces, or enough to keep several pomanders curing at once. This mixture can be used over and over again. Store in a plastic bag between uses.

The finished pomander is a lovely, fragrant thing. If you make lots of them, you can hang a few in closets or linen cupboards. They'll not only scent everything, they'll also help to repel moths (another virtue of cloves).

A pomander should never be discarded. It won't decay; it just hardens and shrinks slightly as it ages. Even when the scent fades, you don't have to throw it away. To renew its fragrance, you can dampen the pomander by dunking it quickly in a bowl of warm water, placing it in a bowl of curing mixture, and covering it with plastic wrap. Turn it each day for several weeks, and your pomander should be as good as new. You may also add a drop of essential oil like cinnamon, allspice, or clove, if desired.

FLORAL WATERS

Floral waters are wonderful and have many uses. Less heavily scented than colognes, they can be used as splashes or toilet waters for a refreshing pick-me-up, or as perfumed additions to baths. But I like them best when they're used to perfume the house. Left uncovered in pretty glass bottles, they subtly scent a bathroom or dressing area. Used in finger bowls at the table, they are delightful, too. When boiled in a saucepan for a few minutes—helped by a nice breeze—floral waters can beautifully perfume several connecting rooms of your home. (By the way, this is also a great idea to try after you've cooked onions, for example, and want to mask the odor. Just boil some whole cloves and a cinnamon stick in water, and the spicy aroma fills the air.)

Essentially, floral waters are a mixture of water, alcohol, fragrant flowers or herbs, and, sometimes, essential oil. They're easy to make at home, and the wonderful bouquet of scent they produce makes the effort well worth your while. Be sure to keep them away from where children or pets can tip them over, however, because they do contain alcohol.

Making Floral Waters

1. When mixing the following recipes, measure out the distilled water (available at pharmacies), then pour into a mixing bottle, making sure the bottle has been thoroughly cleansed.
2. Add the alcohol. Rubbing alcohol won't work, because it contributes a scent of its own to the recipe, so for practical reasons, I've substituted vodka and find that it works just as well.
3. Mix in the flowers (or herbs) so that they're thoroughly wet. Then, if the recipe requires it, add the oil.
4. Let the mixture stand in a covered bottle in a cool, dark place for one week to allow the scent to age.
5. If you like, you can leave the petals or herbs in the mixture for a pretty visual effect. However, some petals don't fare as well as others after they've been through the aging process. If that's the case, just strain them out.

Opposite and above: *Floral waters displayed in old bottles found at summer antiques fairs. The recipes shown include rose water with petals and herbal water with a sprig of rosemary.*

HERBAL WATER

You can use this recipe for making any fragrant flower- or herb-scented water you prefer. I tried it just the other day using dried chamomile flowers, and the result was marvelous.

24 ounces (3 cups) distilled water
2 ounces (¼ cup) vodka
1 ounce dried chamomile flowers, or any flower petals or herbs whose fragrance you prefer

LAVENDER WATER

Lavender Water is not only a delicious bath additive, it's also a terrific way to pick up your spirits on a warm day. Just dip a handkerchief into a batch that you've kept cooling in the refrigerator and pat some onto your face and neck as the Victorians used to do.

16 ounces (2 cups) distilled water
2 ounces (¼ cup) vodka
8 drops lavender oil

FLORIDA WATER

When I was a child, my grandmother always kept a bottle of Florida Water on her dressing table. Although it's still possible to buy it readymade, I always think it's more fun to make my own.

16 ounces (2 cups) distilled water
2 ounces (¼ cup) vodka
6 drops bergamot oil
6 drops lavender oil
2 drops clove oil

ROSE WATER

In ancient times, rose water was sprinkled onto visitors as they entered the house. While this procedure might prove a bit startling for the modern guest, you might consider putting rose water into finger bowls the next time you give a dinner party. Float whole rose heads or petals on top.

16 ounces (2 cups) distilled water
2 ounces (¼ cup) vodka
10 drops rose oil
½ cup fresh, deep-red rose petals

If you have a collection of antique glass bottles, here's an opportunity to put them to good use. If not, any pretty glass bottle or flacon will do, as long as it has a stopper of some kind.

When the floral water has been tinted by the colors of the petals (as in rose water), or if the petals themselves are still in the water, you'll want to show them off in a clear glass bottle. I love bottles clustered together on a table in the bathroom or along a window ledge where they can catch the sunlight. And when you remove the stopper, the contents of the bottle scent the air.

LAVENDER BOTTLES

Nothing can compare with the fresh, clean smell of lavender. When it's in bloom in the summer in our garden, the air is filled with the most enchanting fragrance. It always looks so tidy, growing with its tall straight spikes radiating out in all directions under a deep purple cloud of flower heads. And it's easy to cultivate, thriving in well-drained soil in a sunny location. It makes a beautiful hedge with its silvery foliage. You can also grow lavender in flowerpots in the house. Some people say placed on a window ledge it purifies the air, but in any case it smells wonderful. We grow lots of it and use it in potpourris and flower arrangements in the house. The rest we harvest and sell at Cherchez in bunches and made up into sachets.

In *The Magic of Herbs,* written in 1926 by Mrs. C. F. Leyel, the founder of the Culpeper Herbalists in London, she discusses the intriguing etymology of the word lavender:

The ancients perfumed their baths with the leaves and flowers of lavender, and on that account the word "lavandula" is said to be derived from the Latin "lavare" to wash, and from the custom of putting away freshly washed linen with lavender a washerwoman in the twelfth century was called a lavenderess.

There are other delightful facts as well. The color lavender was the gayest that the Quakers were allowed to wear, and the restorative powers of lavender were held in such esteem that lavender pickers of old used to wear sprigs of the flower under their hats to drive away headaches. Until the beginning of this century lavender was sold in the streets of London. The flower sellers chanted:

Lavender, sweet blooming lavender,
Six bunches a penny today;
Lavender, sweet blooming lavender,
Ladies, buy it while you may.

Even today there are places in Italy and the south of France where you can still buy little sacks of lavender from pushcart vendors who have them heaped in baskets among their fresh flowers.

Lavender is versatile. It always looks pretty in a vase or pitcher even when dried. And after you've used the flower heads (for making potpourri or sachets) you can still make use of the remaining stems which are also very fragrant. Break them up and put them into a muslin sachet for tucking in your linen closet. Or you can tie them into little bundles to burn with kindling in the fireplace. In fact, there isn't one part of the lavender plant that can't be used in one way or another. And one of the prettiest things you can do with bunches of lavender is to make them up into lavender bottles.

A lavender "bottle" is really a bouquet of fragrant lavender flowers encaged in their own stems. I bought one several years ago on a trip to Greece, and was sorry I didn't get more. They're such fun to make, you'll want to do bunches and bunches at a time. They look wonderful massed in a flat basket in a dressing room. Tuck them into closets or armoires. And whenever you press gently against the "cage," you'll release the glorious scent of the flowers within.

When making lavender bottles, it's best to use a lavender variety that's strongly scented and long-stemmed. To avoid some of the confusion that surrounds all the different varieties and types of this plant, I try to buy my seedlings from nurseries specializing in herbs (see the sources at the back of the book). I choose them based on their hardiness as some can be grown only in mild climates. The colors I prefer are usually traditional, from mauves to the deepest purple possible, although lavender also comes in white and pink. My favorites at the moment are Hidcote lavender, which is deep, deep purple and grows to about 15 inches, Munstead, also purple, which grows to about 12 inches, and Grappen

Hall, a taller plant. Whatever varieties of lavender you plant, they can't turn out to be anything but lovely.

Making Lavender Bottles

1. To make one lavender bottle, take about 40 stalks of freshly cut lavender and tie them together with string just below the flower heads. (When picking, leave extra-long stems.) Knot the string tightly enough to hold the stems together without breaking them.

2. Holding the stems upward, carefully bend them back over the heads to make a cage for the buds, arranging them as evenly as possible. (If you can get someone to help you by holding the stems in the center, you can fold them back easily as they fall down around the flower heads.)

3. Using twine or a pretty ribbon, tie the bent stems together just below the flower heads to encase them. Gently knot and tie into a bow.

4. Clip the stems so they're all even.

5. Set the finished lavender bottles flat in a basket and place in a cool, dark closet to dry for a period of several days.

6. After they've dried, take a small, fine-pointed scissors and cut the string which you tied in Step 1. Pull it out and discard.

Fresh lavender in an old English trug

*Lavender bottles in the making.
After stems are tied beneath the
buds, they are pulled down over the
buds and tied to form
a "cage" for them.
Opposite: A dozen lavender bottles
placed in a flat wooden tray
ready for drying.*

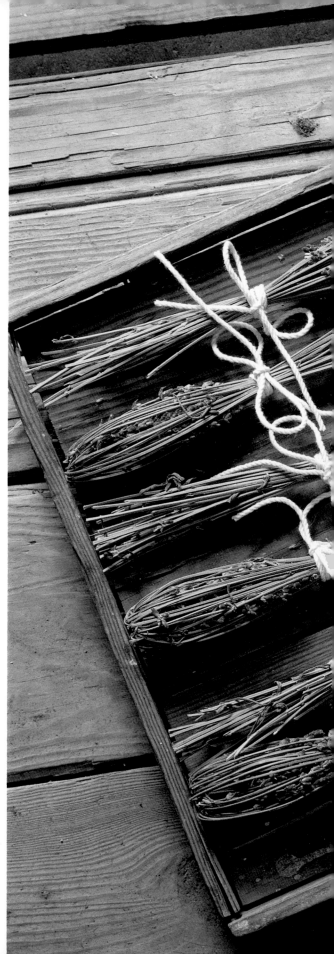

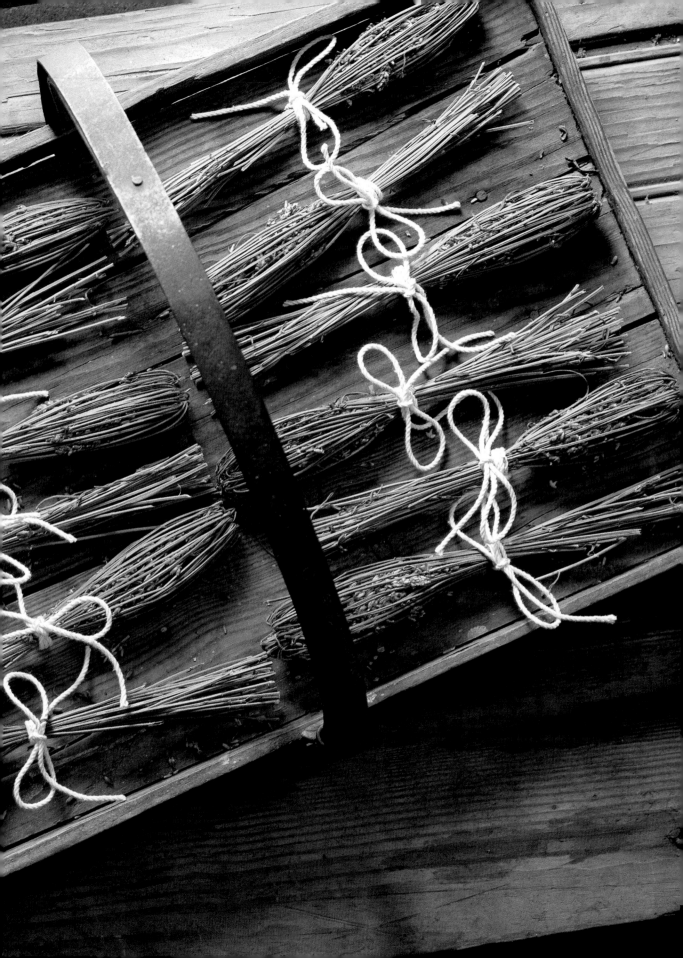

4
OTHER SCENTS

All the scenting ideas I've discussed so far—potpourris, sachets, pomanders, and so on—are things that you can make yourself in order to add fragrance to a room. However, there are other methods that can also be used. Most would be impossible to make yourself, but all should be considered when scenting a home.

Almost every day, someone walks into Cherchez to ask our advice about specific scent problems. This is especially problematic in urban areas where apartments are heated in winter, air-conditioned in summer—and windows are closed most of the time. My first suggestion is always to open the doors and windows and give the house or apartment a good old-fashioned airing. The fresh air sweeps through the rooms like a new broom and the staleness disappears. Then it's time to enrich your environment by adding fragrance.

Although I prefer using the old-fashioned, natural methods whenever I can —like throwing a handful of cloves and some cinnamon sticks into boiling water until the wonderful, spicy aroma fills the house—there are times when newer fragrance forms can be invaluable and really quite lovely.

Room sprays, scented candles, perfume lamps, incense, essential oils, all can be used separately or in conjunction with the things you've made to scent all the rooms in your home. In addition, many can successfully mask problems such as pet smells, tobacco smoke, mildew, mustiness, lingering food odors—all the smells to which the average household can be prone at one time or another. Most are available in fragrance or herb shops or in stores that carry better fragrances for the home. (See source guide at the end of the book.)

Above: *Scented candles massed on a sideboard make
a wonderful greeting for party guests.* Opposite: *Pine
cones dotted with fragrant essential oil and bundles of
lavender and rosemary branches tied with string. Toss
them into your fire along with the burning logs
and see how they scent the room.*

Room Sprays. These can be a highly effective way of scenting a room or area because they work immediately. With several spurts you can quickly fill the air with fragrance. Room sprays are also great for combating cooking, tobacco, and pet odors in any room, large or small. I always keep a can in each room so it's handy when needed. Be particular when choosing your room sprays. A scent that is appropriate in your kitchen or bathroom may not be sophisticated enough for other living spaces.

A room spray doesn't have to be confined to the house. Stash one in the glove compartment to freshen the air inside a car, or use it in the cabin of a boat. Room sprays, by their very nature, don't last very long, so if you want a long-lasting fragrance, you may have to use them in conjunction with something else, like a scented candle. Just make sure that the scents are the same or at least compatible. Your own nose will be the best judge.

Drawer Liners. This more familiar scent form has always been popular, perhaps because it appeals to the neatness instinct in all of us. There's something very satisfying about a drawer that's been freshly straightened and lined with pretty, scented paper. Although drawer liners can also be made of fabric, I use the paper kind and usually add one or two sachets to each drawer for good measure. Either way, they're also great for lining the tops of closet shelves and the insides of chests, or for covering the shelves of an armoire or a linen cupboard. Drawer liner papers are often so nicely designed, you may even want to use them to line the insides of any little antique boxes you may have.

Essential Oils. The oils used in making and refreshing potpourris and sachets are highly concentrated forms of scent usually called essential oils. Unlike cologne or toilet waters, they do not have any alcohol added and are therefore stronger smelling and longer lasting. Put a drop on the light bulb of a strategically placed lamp and the heat of the bulb will diffuse the lovely scent throughout the room. In our shop, we have special copper rings just for this purpose. You place a drop of oil in the trough of the ring and place the ring atop the bulb. In this case, the heated copper acts as the scent conductor.

Another nice way to use essential oil is to dot some onto a cotton ball and rub it into the inside of wood drawers. The wood will absorb the oil, which in turn will scent the contents of the drawer. Use this same method for adding fragrance to storage trunks and wooden blanket chests, or rub some onto the underside of a table next to the sofa. I've even put a few scented drops onto the grille of my air conditioner (a cotton swab makes a good applicator for this) and enjoyed my favorite fragrance whenever the cooling system was turned on.

During most of the year, our home is filled with flower fragrances—single scents such as heliotrope, lilac, tuberose, jasmine, lily of the valley, or mixed essences. But you have a lot to choose from as essential oils come in a vast array of floral scents from bergamot to wisteria and in other ranges including citrus, spice, and woodsy ones.

During the winter months—at Christmastime especially—I like to drop some essential oil onto the pine cones I collect in a basket next to the fireplace. Then I burn the cones with the kindling —and you can imagine the heavenly fragrance *that* produces. Our spicy lavender oil is my favorite to use. Other good choices are cinnamon and balsam.

Incense. Like candles, incense burns slowly and leaves a lasting fragrance impression. I prefer candles to incense, as candles tend to have a cleaner, less smoky smell. Again, it's a matter of personal taste. However, I do like the idea of burning a bunch of fragrant twigs in the fireplace. As you harvest lavender, basil, rosemary, and mints, save the stems for this purpose. Just tie them up with string into fat bundles after they have dried and toss one or two onto the fire with the kindling wood.

Aromatic Diffusers. These are usually small vases or vials made of clay that are either partly glazed or not glazed at all. You put your essential oil into the vase, sealing it with a cork. The oil slowly diffuses into the air through the pottery. They are usually quite attractive looking and are small enough for dressing tables or bathrooms where counter space is limited.

Scented Candles. These impart fragrance that's strong and pervasive, and therefore create a special mood. Scented candles must be well made and very fragrant in order to be effective. If they smell strong in the store without being lit, then they should scent effectively when you get them home. The fragrance is long-lasting, permeating the air and the porous materials in the room, such as fabric and wood. I like to use clusters of candles on tables in the living room and in foyers and halls.

Needless to say, you always have to keep an eye on burning candles. I let mine burn only for short periods of time, but the beautiful scent lingers on.

When it comes to choosing a candle fragrance, I prefer a mixed floral. But as I've said before, it's a very individual matter, so choose a candle scent the way you would a potpourri or a perfume—to suit your own taste.

Perfume Burning Lamps. I first saw this idea used in Europe, but now you can buy these lamps here in this country. It consists of a glass or china container, which holds scented oil. At the top there is a wick and a stone burner. You light the lamp for a short period of time, extinguish it, and the fragrance it produces continues to fill the room. Its advantage is that it does not need to be kept lit for long periods of time.

Scented Burning Papers. This idea has always intrigued me. When we were in Florence one spring, we visited a place called Santa Maria Novella which looks much as it did when it was started as a convent in 1612. Today it functions as a family-owned pharmacy, and within its magnificent marble walls they carry a serendipitous variety of things. Among my favorite finds there were scented papers. If you burn one of these blotter-weight paper slips in an ashtray or saucer, it fills the air with a hauntingly beautiful fragrance.

Decorating

Your Home

5
WREATHS

The delightful thing about dried flowers is that they enable us to enjoy the lushness and beauty of live flowers throughout the year. In the dead of winter, when a variety of flowers is harder to find, you can take all of the leaves and blossoms you dried the summer before and use them to fill baskets and vases throughout the house. Or make them up into wreaths. Wreaths look especially pretty hanging above a sideboard or on a door (inside or out) and always add a touch of color and texture that only flowers and leaves can bring to a room.

Even in the summer, when the fresh flowers in your garden can be picked by the armful, dried wreaths still work beautifully as accents. They're also nice in a second home. When you arrive there for the weekend—before you've had time to even think about picking flowers—you'll have some wreaths already in place to provide a cheery welcome.

Wreaths make the kind of gift that everyone seems to love. The ones you make yourself are even more appreci-

ated, and since all the botanicals used in a wreath are dried, you can make several at a time to have on hand when an occasion arises.

There are many different kinds of wreaths you can make, but I prefer two especially: flower wreaths, which are very colorful and rich looking with lots of flowers, and herb wreaths made from leaves of different textures and a variety of monochromatic colors. In addition, you can use the same wreath directions I give below to make other things—like a candle wreath, which lies flat on a table around the base of a candlestick (great for dinner parties and buffets). Or you can make garlands and wreaths to wear, which look beautiful in place of hats or veils at a country wedding or other festive occasions.

Whatever type of wreath you decide to make, you'll find that as decoration it can be as versatile as a painting. I'll sometimes take a picture off the wall and replace it with a flower or herb wreath just for a nice change.

Opposite: *A welcoming dried flower wreath hanging on a door includes peonies, lemon leaves, larkspur, and yellow roses.* Above: *Smaller candle wreaths of princess pine and globe amaranth surround the bases of cut glass candlesticks and act as a centerpiece for settings of old Wedgwood shell dishes and gleaming family silver.*

Even before you gather the materials needed for making a wreath, there are a few points you'll want to keep in mind.

Color. This is an important factor. If you intend to make a flower wreath, for example, you'll have to decide whether you want your palette to be multicolored or monochromatic. For an herb wreath, you may want to create a high contrast by using very dark greens played against lighter greens or grays. Or keep the wreath only dark or light. You may even want to expand your color range by adding berries, seed heads, mosses, or barks. Whatever you decide, the colors of the wreath should always coordinate with the colors of the room in which it will be placed.

Sizes and Shapes. You should use various botanicals of different sizes. For a flower wreath, you'll want to select flowers that have been dried in different stages of growth, from bud to full blown. Varying the depth at which you place the elements is another way of adding interest to the overall shape of the wreath.

Textures. Variety in texture can be achieved easily by mixing in seedpods with barks, lacy flowers with densely clustered blossoms, leaves that are flat and shiny along with others that are textured and matte, and so on. The contrast will contribute to the individuality of the wreath you create.

Ribbons. You may want to add a beautiful ribbon or other trimming to give your wreath a "fussier" look. Again, whatever trim you choose, be sure that it coordinates.

Seasons of the Year. Depending on the botanical elements used, a wreath can be a lovely addition to the home during holiday festivities. It can echo the blazing, golden tones of autumn, or the multicolored glories of spring.

Fragrance. By putting a few drops of your favorite essential oil under the leaves or base of a wreath, you can scent the area of the room in which it is hung. You will then need to refresh it with oil every so often, to keep the area fragrant.

HERB WREATHS

Here are the materials you'll need:

A straw form (the finished wreath will be 2 to 4 inches larger than the form, so choose the size accordingly).

Florist's pins, to attach the herbs to the form.

Sprigs of four kinds of dried herbs, 5 inches long. Use opal basil, Silver King artemisia, parsley, and sage or another combination with nice color contrast, such as lamb's ears, rosemary, Silver Lace artemisia, and tansy.

A wire loop, for hanging the wreath.

Making an Herb Wreath

1. Starting with the Silver King artemisia (or the lightest-colored herb), arrange several sprigs, stems outward, to create a curved row on the form. Attach each sprig to the form with florist's pins.
2. Create a second and third row with the rest of the artemisia so that the three rows are equidistant from each other. Pin in place as before. Be sure to keep all sprigs curving in the same direction and to overlap the sprigs to hide the pins.
3. Alongside each row of the artemisia and using the same technique, make three rows each of the opal basil and the parsley or whatever herbs give the highest color contrast to the first. Then add the sage or darkest herbs. You should now have twelve rows in all on the form.

4. Attach the wire loop to the back of the wreath for hanging.

FLOWER WREATHS

Here are the materials you'll need:

A *straw form or Styrofoam form* (available at most garden centers and local craft stores). When choosing a form, remember that the finished wreath will be 2 to 4 inches larger than the form itself.

Craft wire, 22- or 24-gauge, for attaching the greens and making a wire loop for hanging the wreath.

Floral tape, self-adhesive, about ¼ inch wide.

Craft glue, fast-drying.

Dried background greens with stems. These will cover the front and sides of the wreath form and should be flexible, not brittle. Good choices would include Silver King artemisia, sage, boxwood, eucalyptus, leatherleaf fern, Spanish moss, princess pine, and lamb's ears.

Dried flower heads such as peony, rose, larkspur, tansy, yarrow, statice, cornflower, lily, iris, lavender, hollyhock, or globe amaranth.

Decorative ribbon (optional).

Making a Flower Wreath

1. Layer the greens around the front of the form, wrapping and anchoring them with wire so the greens overlap and cover the sides as well. Add another layer of greens and wrap as before until the entire form is covered. Finish off the background greens by tucking the stems of the last row under tops of the first row.

2. Experimentally place the dried flower heads around the wreath to determine the most pleasing arrangement. Then carefully apply glue to the base of each flower and gently press it onto the greens. To keep the wreath from looking too stiff, place the flowers in random directions and at slightly different depths. Lift the greens slightly as you go so the flowers look nested into them as if growing from them naturally.

3. Add decorative ribbons and essential oil if desired.

4. Make a loop from the wire (for hanging) and attach it to the back of the wreath or ribbon.

Although dried wreaths generally last a long time, they won't last forever. And when a wreath finally begins to look faded or even slightly bedraggled, just discard it (you can still recycle the wreath form and make another one). Until that time, however, there are things you can do to keep your wreath looking as fresh and pretty as it was meant to:

❧ Never place a wreath in direct sunlight.
❧ Avoid placing it in a room that's very humid.
❧ Every so often, dust it gently with an artist's soft, watercolor brush.
❧ At different times of the year, you may want to store your wreath away for a time. Do so in an airtight container with a handful of silica gel to absorb moisture. Place the container in a dark, cool closet.

Three steps in making an herb wreath. Left: *The straw form.* Right: *Sprigs of artemisia and opal basil arranged in three curved rows with floral pins.* Below: *Layers of parsley and sage are added to finish.*

Three steps in making a flower wreath. Left: *The greens layered around the straw form.* Right: *The flowers glued and gently pressed on in random directions.* Below: *The finished wreath, a beautiful blaze of color.*

6
BOUQUETS

A year or so after we moved into our house in the country, we still hadn't the time to start a flower garden, and there wasn't a florist for miles around. But we did have an herb garden. So whenever we visited friends, we'd bring an herb bouquet. I'd pick parsley, sweet basil, lemon thyme and verbena, chive and tarragon, sage, various kinds of mint, and perhaps a sprig of rosemary. Then I'd tie the fresh bouquet with thick twine and wrap it all up in kraft paper. It was a special gift from a country garden which always delighted everyone who received it. It could be put in a vase, hung on a door to dry, or used for cooking.

I love the unexpected. A bouquet doesn't always have to mean fresh flowers, although many people tend to think so. Bouquets can be made of flowers, herbs, or even branches of leaves and tall grasses. They can be fresh or dried. I love giving them. My favorites include tussie-mussies and door bouquets. They make beautiful additions to any home—whether your own or a friend's.

TUSSIE-MUSSIES

This little nosegay of flowers and herbs is a wonderful way to express your sentiments to someone on a special occasion or on one you'd like to make special. In the eighteenth century, tussie-mussies were carried around the house for health reasons (their perfume was believed to cleanse the air), but in the nineteenth century, they were customarily given as tokens of affection, and each sprig in the bouquet was chosen to represent a specific message. Rosemary (for remembrance) might be included for someone about to go on a journey, or forget-me-nots (true love) in a bouquet intended for a sweetheart.

A tussie-mussie can be made from any flowers you prefer. But if you'd like to make the classic message bouquet, here's a sample list of flowers and herbs and their definitions. They vary slightly from book to book, so the following is only one version. If you're especially interested in the subject, you may want to track down one of the old flower language books or buy a modern one to supplement the vocabulary I've given here.

The giving of tussie-mussies is a charming old tradition that we can still practice today—whether the elements in the bouquet deliver a message or not. They can be made of dried flowers and herbs, which is the way we do them at Cherchez, or of fresh flowers from the garden.

They make wonderful gifts, and since they last a long time, you can make several at once. They're perfect as a

Greens inserted into a paper doily act as a base for the flowers.

Placing the bouquet in a glass will hold it upright while you glue on the dried flower heads.

The finished tussie-mussie

Left: A dried tussie-mussie makes a perfect Valentine's Day gift.

going-away gift or for cheering up some-one in the hospital. They can also make a very special present look more special when tied to the top of the box with a ribbon.

To make a tussie-mussie, you will need the following materials:

2 round white paper doilies, 6 inches in diameter.
floral tape, ¼-inch wide, self-adhesive.
1 yard of ribbon, ¼-inch wide.
background greens, such as artemisia, box, lamb's ears, santolina or other herb sprigs, with stems 3 inches long.
1 rose (a traditional tussie-mussie always has a rose in the center).
an assortment of 6–9 flower heads (see flower list, p. 92).
craft glue, fast-drying.

Making a Tussie-Mussie

1. Fold one doily in half, then in quarters, and continue folding in that manner to create a fluted effect. Cut a hole in the center of the doily.
2. Take 3 or 4 pieces of greens and slip the stems through the doily hole. Trim the stems at the bottom so they come to a point.
3. Starting at the base of the doily, wrap and stretch floral tape around the stems from top to bottom. Cut excess tape. Set upright in a cup or jar.
4. Apply the glue to the base of the rose and place in the center of the tussie-mussie. Press down gently to secure.
5. Apply glue to the base of the other flower heads and arrange them so they're evenly spaced in a circle around the center rose. Press each one down gently to secure in place as you go.
6. Flute the second doily as described in Step 1. Cut a hole through the center and slip the stems of the tussie-mussie through.

7. To keep the doilies in place, wrap ribbon around the stems once or twice at the base of the doilies, then double-knot and tie into a bow.
8. Many people like to add a drop or two of a floral essential oil as a finishing touch. Dab it on the ribbon in a place where it will not show.

DOOR BOUQUETS

This is another way of bringing the delights of your garden into the house and enjoying them the year round. Unlike the more structured tussie-mussie, a door bouquet is an informal massing of dried flowers, leaves, herbs, and grasses, all tied together with a length of twine or string. The effect is spontaneous and random-looking. If you don't have a garden, you can use wild flowers and grasses for this type of arrangement.

The important thing is to select a nice variety of textures and colors that work well against each other. One example of such a combination might include flowers you have dried in silica gel, on their stems, such as peonies and lilacs. Another choice might be the herbs and the greens in the southernwood/lavender bouquet for which I've given directions below. I like to hang a bunch of these on my closet doors.

When I bunch my door bouquet elements together, I use layers of varying lengths and make a graduated arrangement with the shortest stems on top and the longest on the bottom. That way, when I hang it up, I can see all the different botanicals in the bouquet. Door bouquets can be hung over the top of a mirror in a hallway or tied to the tops of bedposts. To hang one on a front door at Christmastime is festive and fragrant!

CLOSET DOOR BOUQUET

Aside from its decorative value, a door bouquet can be put to good use. With that in mind, here are directions for making a bouquet that deters moths and insects. Hang it on the outside of a closet door or hook it over the doorknob.

1. Take 1 full, long-stemmed sprig each of tansy, wormwood, southernwood, lav-ender, Silver King artemisia, and rose-mary. Air-dry following the directions given on page 105.

2. Arrange the dried sprigs in a bunch with the shortest stems on top. Fasten them tightly together with a rubber band.

3. Knot a length of twine over the rubber band and wind the twine around the stems for about 1½ inches to hide the rubber band. Knot twine a second time and make a bow or loop.

 ## THE LANGUAGE OF FLOWERS

FLOWER OR HERB	MEANING
Amaranth (globe)	*unfading love*
Angelica	*inspiration*
Balm	*sympathy*
Bluebell	*constancy*
Chrysanthemum (red)	*I love*
Clover (white)	*think of me*
Daffodil	*regard*
Daisy	*innocence*
Dock	*patience*
Forget-Me-Not	*true love; forget me not*
Garden Chervil	*sincerity*
Geranium (rose-scented)	*preference*
Heliotrope	*devotion, a person's faithfulness*
Hibiscus	*delicate beauty*
Hollyhock	ambition
Honeysuckle	*generous and devoted affection*
Jonquil	*I desire a return of affection*
Larkspur	*lightness, levity*
Lilac (purple)	*first emotions of love*
Lilac (white)	*youthful innocence*
Lily (white)	*purity, sweetness*
Lily-of-the-Valley	*return of happiness*

FLOWER OR HERB	MEANING
Magnolia	*love of nature*
Mignonette	*your qualities surpass your charms*
Mimosa	*sensitiveness*
Mint	*virtue*
Mugwort	*happiness*
Nasturtium	*patriotism*
Pansy	*thinking of you*
Parsley	*festivity*
Peppermint	*warmth of feeling*
Periwinkle (blue)	*early friendship*
Periwinkle (white)	*pleasures of memory*
Ranunculus	*you are radiant with charms*
Rose	*love*
Rose (red and white together)	*unity*
Rosebud (red)	*pure and lovely*
Rosemary	*remembrance*
Sage (garden)	*esteem*
Sorrel	*affection*
Spearmint	*warmth of sentiment*
Stock	*lasting beauty*
Sweet Basil	*good wishes*
Violet (blue)	*faithfulness*
White Jasmine	*amiableness*
Woodbine	*fraternal love*
Zinnia	*thoughts of an absent friend*

A door bouquet made from herbs and leaves and tied onto a bedpost

Above left and right: *Door bouquets can look elegant or countrified.*
Opposite: *An herb bouquet picked from our country garden*

7

FLOWER ARRANGEMENTS

The longer I garden, the more convinced I become that flowers are most precious—and so very necessary for our well-being. One of the greatest joys of working with flowers comes in spring and summer, when we can fill vases, pitchers, and even simple jelly jars to overflowing with flowers freshly cut from our garden. It is a fragrant feast for the eye and the mind as well. The way they change and enrich a room is always an unexpected surprise. Even a random bunch of wild flowers picked by a little nephew looks wonderful sitting on a windowsill in its kitchen glass.

I love flowers, and I love to live with them all year long. As the end of the summer rolls around, the prospect of filling antique baskets and vases with masses of dried flowers is a delightful challenge. How I look forward to those first rainy weekends in early autumn. That's when I enjoy taking stock of the abundance of flowers, leaves, and other materials I've dried. I believe there is a place for both fresh and dried flowers in our homes. And, in fact, both can be used at the same time to enhance our surroundings.

Flower arranging is an art, and many wonderful books have been written on the subject. I like to browse through my favorite ones often, picking up gems of information, ideas, and inspiration at the same time.

It's a continual source of pleasure for me when I see what the Dutch and Flemish flower painters were doing in the seventeenth century, or how the French painters approached flower still lifes in the eighteenth century. The different views generate new ideas.

Some of the favorites in our collec-

Dutch paintings inspired this lush arrangement of dried flowers, which includes peonies, delphiniums, tulips, lilies, daisies, tree peony leaves, and astilbe. The perfect vase—a cast-iron garden urn.

Three steps for making a flower arrangement with wild and cultivated flowers: Queen Anne's lace, goldenrod, zinnia, globe amaranth, and pearly everlasting.

tion of flower and garden books include *The Art of Flower Arrangement,* by Beverley Nichols; *The Gracious Art of Flower Arrangement,* by Susan Pulbrook and Rosamund Gould; *Flowers in House and Garden,* by Constance Spry; *The History of Flower Arrangement,* by Julia S. Berrall; and there are many good contemporary ones as well. In books like these you will find not only ideas, but also some valuable information on the hows and whys of flower arranging. Many of the older books are out of print but are often available in public and horticultural society libraries. You can also buy them, as I have, from booksellers that specialize in antiquarian, rare, and out-of-print books. Most of them keep request lists and will call you whenever a book you want comes in. (For more information, see source guide, Antiquarian Booksellers, page 127.) Now here are a few tips that I've picked up along the way.

The first thing to remember when you begin a dried flower arrangement is that it's not a test. Don't rush yourself. All the materials you'll be working with are dried, which means that some may be delicate or brittle, and you will see that working with dried flowers is very different from working with live ones. Take your time. You must have patience and work carefully, stopping every now and then to take a good look at the composition in progress.

Second, don't let yourself feel too constricted by the "rules" about what you should and shouldn't do. Let your imagination go and allow the natural character of the flowers themselves to direct you. Don't be afraid to be creative—your raw materials are already so beautiful!

Constance Spry was an extraordinary woman whose knowledge of flowers and gardens is legendary. Her innovative flower arrangements encompassed all growing things: flowers, leaves, branches, and even vegetables, and her books are filled with ideas. Here, in *Constance Spry's Garden Notebook,* published in 1940, one gets to hear a nice little bit of her flower philosophy:

I feel so strongly that the art of flower arrangement should be a means of self expression for everyone and that nobody should be afraid to express his feeling for color and line through this medium. . . . Do what you please, follow your own star. . . . Just be natural and gay and light hearted and pretty and simple and overflowing and general and baroque and bare and austere and stylized and wild and daring and conservative, and learn and learn and learn. Open your hearts to every form of beauty.

But where do you start? Generally I prefer floral bouquets with a diversity of color. So I always decide on the colors first, then I select the specific flowers and greens. The colors you choose will depend largely on the colors of the room in which you intend to place the finished arrangement. Like a painting, it should be treated as a decorative element, and when the colors of the arrangement are right, it can add greatly to the feeling and appearance of the room. The opposite is also true. An uncoordinated flower arrangement can be an extremely discordant element in a room. Which brings me to my favorite subject. When live flowers start to fade or look unattractive, we discard them immediately. Why then do many people let a faded, dry, brownish old dried arrangement sit there forever getting dustier and dustier? Dried flowers do not last forever and are not meant to.

In an earlier chapter on wreaths and the dried materials used to make them, I discussed the importance of color, texture, depth, and contrast. To those, add the element of composition. Because your arrangement will be three-dimensional, balance is crucial. And by that I

don't mean formality or symmetry, but rather a flowing composition that looks natural and spontaneous.

The other thing to consider is light. Where do you plan to put your arrangement? In a room with natural light or in a corner or alcove where it will undoubtably have to be artificially lit? Or will it be candlelit as a centerpiece on a table might be? This should be decided at the outset since it will affect what colors and intensities of colors you pick.

The container you use should be carefully chosen so that it suits both the flowers and the setting in which the final arrangement will be placed. Vases, cachepots, baskets, pitchers, or bowls could all work. In fact, any number of receptacles, whether old or new, whether of china, glass, pottery, silver, or brass, would do. The deciding factor will be your own individual taste.

As for size, good sense should act as your guide. A centerpiece arrangement, for example, has to be low enough to allow your guests to see one another across the table, while one on a sideboard should be proportionate to the furniture piece itself without overwhelming it or getting lost on it.

A final word: When first starting out, you'd do best to work on a small, simple arrangement. You can end up with a little gem and have fun doing it while you learn from the experience. Then, after honing your skills, you can go on to bigger and better things.

To assemble a flower arrangement, you'll need the following materials:

A container.

Floral foam low to medium density (the kind used for dried flower arranging).

Assorted dried greens, herbs, or grasses of your choice.

Assorted dried flower heads.

Assorted dried flowers with wire stems. (See Chapter 9 for directions on how to dry stemmed flowers.)

Craft glue, fast drying.

Making a Flower Arrangement

1. Cut a piece of floral foam into a rectangular shape so that it fits snugly into the container and rises 2 inches above the top of it. The extra height will allow you to insert the greens and flowers so that they cascade gracefully. (When the dried materials have all been inserted, the foam will not be visible.) Using a table knife, diagonally slice the pointy corners from the top of the foam so that it's somewhat spherical in shape.

2. Poke the greens into the foam starting at the top, then working down the sides. The stems of the greens should be inserted to their halfway point so the arrangement is secure.

3. Next, insert the wire-stemmed flowers. To avoid a pincushion effect, insert the flowers so some are higher than others. Keep the larger flowers toward the bottom and use the smaller ones at the top.

4. Finally, apply glue to dried flower heads and carefully press them into the arrangement wherever they look most effective.

5. If desired, the arrangement can be scented by dabbing essential oil on the underside of the greens.

Working with Flowers

8

GROWING
& GATHERING

Your finished potpourri, wreath, or bouquet will only be as beautiful as the botanicals used to make it, so in this chapter I will be talking about what flowers and herbs to grow for the best results and how to properly harvest them for drying purposes. Great care should be taken to ensure that the dried flowers and leaves you use are always pretty and fresh-looking and that the colors are as close to their original predried state as possible. Not all flowers look pretty when dried, and it helps to know which ones will and which won't before you attempt to preserve them by drying.

I've been experimenting with flower drying for about ten years now, and after many failures and successes I've compiled the following list of flowers that always look beautiful when dried, keep a good deal of their original color, and won't disappoint. They're the ones I rely on for making dried wreaths, flower arrangements, and various bouquets, and I use the flower heads for decorating the tops of big bowls of potpourri. Also, the petals of some of these flowers are perfect for making the potpourri itself, and these are marked with a small leaf symbol next to them. You may recognize some of them from the potpourri recipes given earlier in this book, but I've included additional flowers in case you want to experiment with recipes of your own.

Whether you choose to grow these flowers or buy them fresh from a florist to dry at home (see Chapter 9 on drying), or even if you buy them already dried from a botanical supplier, use this list as a guide and you won't be disappointed with the result.

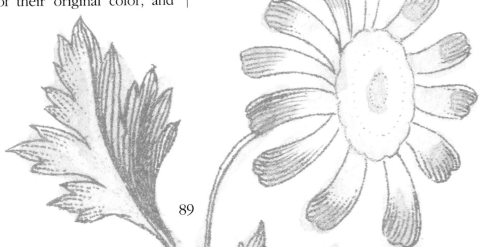

Ironstone pitchers filled with larkspur, snapdragon, nigella, shrub roses, and monkshood

China pitchers with flower motifs make lovely vases for cut flowers.

Left: *Sweet cicely, Silver Lace artemisia, and sage in my collection of hand-blown and cut glass pitchers*

FLOWERS TO DRY

ageratum, golden

ammobium

anemone ❧

aster

astilbe

baby's breath

bellflower ❧

calendula ❧

carnation ❧

celosia

cornflower ❧

coxcomb

daffodil ❧

dahlia

daisy

delphinium ❧

forget-me-not

foxglove

freesia

geranium, scented ❧

gerbera

globe amaranth ❧

hibiscus ❧

hollyhock

honeysuckle

hydrangea

iris ❧

jasmine

jonquil ❧

larkspur ❧

lavender ❧

lilac

lily ❧

lily-of-the-valley

marigold ❧

monkshood

nasturtium

orange blossom

pansy

peony ❧

petunia

pinks ❧

ranunculus

rose ❧

salvia ❧

sea holly

statice

stock ❧

strawflower ❧

sunflower ❧

sweet pea

sweet rocket

tulip

veronica

violet ❧

yarrow

zinnia

❧ *flowers especially suitable for potpourri*

In addition to flowers, you can use lots of other dried materials such as leaves, seed heads, and herbs. Below are the most useful ones to help get you started. Most of the leaves can be air-dried and used on their stems in dried flower arrangements or in wreaths. Leaves that have a leaf symbol next to them can be picked off the stems for use in potpourri.

If the choice seems somewhat limited, it's because so many leaves tend to turn a stale-colored green when dried. But I'm always picking up leaves and seed heads from here and there and drying them to discover something new, and the following represent those botanicals which have given me the best results.

LEAVES TO DRY

bay leaf ❧

box ❧

eucalyptus ❧

fern

lemon leaves

rose leaf

scotch broom

tree peony leaf

wild grasses

❧ *leaves especially suitable for potpourri*

SEED HEADS TO DRY

foxglove

iris

leek

nigella

onion

poppy

Even if you don't have a garden of your own, you can find any number of wonderful plants growing in meadows or along roadsides that can be used in making dried flower arrangements. (Just be sure to check out which plants are protected by conservation laws in your state before you pick.) Even a simple branch found on the ground can be a beautiful addition. Experiment. Be creative. Dry a sprig or two of what you've found, and you may be pleasantly surprised at the result. Some good examples are given in the list below. They're all to be found in the wild, and all can be used successfully for flower arrangements.

WILD FLOWERS TO DRY

black-eyed Susan	pearly everlasting
dock	pussy willow
goldenrod (in bud)	Queen Anne's lace
Joe-Pye weed	teasel
loosestrife	thistle

So far we've been talking about the visual impact of the botanicals you select for your projects, but there's another aspect to consider, too, and that is their scent. If you're in the process of planning a garden (or would like to add to the one you already have), you might want to consider introducing herbs, which are not only physically beautiful but fragrant as well. In *The Herb Garden,* by Frances A. Bardswell (published in England in 1930), the author says:

Considering how large a part the visible plays in our enjoyment of gardens, it is not a little surprising to notice how much of their charm also depends on the invisible.... Scent is less explainable, less definable, and its wonders have been less explored. There are few better places for the study of scents than the herb garden.

Herbs are fairly easy to grow, so if you have even a small but sunny spot, I would encourage you to cultivate an herb garden. The most sensible way of starting is to buy some seedlings. That way, you can see and smell each plant first before selecting the varieties you prefer.

There are many styles of herb gardens, from the informal with herbs and flowers growing side by side and blending into one another (like ours), to knot gardens with hedges planted in a formal design. Whichever you choose, unless you have help, it's a good idea to start with a manageable number of plants. You can always add more as the growing season progresses. Each year we add more varieties of plants to our garden, trying new things as we go along.

Most of the herbs we grow in our garden are perennials—which means they reappear each year as if by magic—and we supplement them with our favorite annuals which we plant every spring. In the following list, you'll find herbs we grow for potpourri (the ones with the leaf symbol next to them) as well as for other dried flower projects. Many leafy herbs, such as artemisia, sage, and rosemary, can work wonderfully in wreaths, tussie-mussies, and flower arrangements as well as potpourri.

HERBS TO DRY

borage	mint ❧
catmint	mugwort
chamomile ❧	pot marjoram
costmary ❧	rosemary ❧
fennel	rue
feverfew ❧	sage ❧
flax	salvia ❧
germander	Silver King artemisia ❧
heliotrope	
hyssop	Silver Lace artemisia ❧
lady's-mantle	
lamb's ears ❧	southernwood ❧
lavender (cotton)	sweet cicely
lavender (English) ❧	sweet woodruff ❧
lavender (French) ❧	tansy
lemon balm ❧	thyme ❧
lemon verbena ❧	wormwood

❧ *herbs especially suitable for potpourri*

Russell Page, one of the most influential of our contemporary landscape designers, wrote a book (a must in any gardener's library) called *The Education of a Gardener,* in which he says: "I suppose that your true gardener considers his gardening as a personal pleasure and a private struggle, although I never knew one who would not enjoy showing and sharing his successes."

Tarragon and thyme in the herb garden

Larkspur planted in front of marigolds

Foxglove planted at the edge of a wood

Flowers that will be harvested for drying

Hidcote lavender in bloom in our garden

A profusion of black-eyed Susans in a garden

Herbs forming a border for a lily pond

Borage just before it comes into bloom

If you've never planted a garden before but feel inspired to do so after seeing all the wonderful things you can do with dried flowers, I urge you to study a few of your friends' gardens or to visit a good public garden or two before you plant a seed. They can give you some useful ideas, and it's a good chance to see what your plants will actually look like after they've grown. (See page 123 for a list of my favorite gardens to visit.)

GATHERING

Timing is key to the successful gathering of your homegrown flowers, herbs, and leaves for drying. This means that you should pick them on a dry, sunny day after a day of good weather, preferably in the morning after the dew has evaporated. Because dampness slows the drying process and inhibits color retention, it's very important that the botanicals you pick be as dry as possible.

Aside from that, the question of when to gather will depend on what you're gathering. Tulips and daffodils, of course, are springtime blooms, but almost everything else will be gathered in summer—and that means most of the summer, as each variety of plant reaches its peak of perfection. Be discerning. You'll want to gather only the most beautiful flower heads, petals, and leaves that you can find—those which have the most pleasing shapes and colors and no blemishes. This means that you'll have to keep an eye on everything as it grows so you'll know what will be ripe for picking and when. For example, I harvest rosemary and sage all summer long, but I only gather pot marjoram when the dark-purple blooms come out and the buds are very slightly opened.

It's very handy to have your garden accessible. In *The English Flower Garden* and *Home Grounds* (1883), William Robinson said:

In olden times, so far as any evidence remains to us from pictures, prints, tapestries, etc., the place for the flower garden was quite near the house; and that is the place for it now. In the best conditions, it should be like an extension of the house—a larger flower room.

As for the amount you harvest from such a garden, that will depend on how much help you have available or on how much you can manage to do yourself, because everything you pick must be prepared for drying and preferably on the same day. We have lots of lavender planted in our gardens—and luckily, a houseful of family and friends in summer who love to help us gather it. (Gathering plants is a wonderful project that the whole family can enjoy doing together.) Sometimes at six o'clock in the morning, I'll look out the window and see one of my young nieces in the herb garden looking intently at the lavender to see if this is *the* day. And if it is—if the flower buds have reached the deep purple but not-quite-open stage—then we'll all spend the next three or four days picking and drying lavender.

Once the gathering season starts, you'll find that the following tools and accessories will be put to good use:

Sharp garden shears.

Florist scissors and/or a sharp knife.

Gardening gloves.

Old sheets or tablecloths for sorting out the harvest.

Several metal or plastic water buckets.

Baskets for carrying what you've gathered. We have a whole collection of baskets used just for this purpose. It includes

American herb baskets and our collection of English trugs. Flat baskets are great for gathering, too.

It's important to be as organized as possible when you harvest your flowers and leaves. As a general rule, we harvest one thing at a time. It's less confusing that way, and in midsummer, when so many things are ready to be picked at the same time, it helps simplify matters.

Everything you gather should be brought to a central place for sorting. We sometimes use our back porch for this task, covering the floor with an old tablecloth to catch the flower heads that fall off. How you sort the various plants you've picked will depend on what you intend to use them for later.

As you cut each big bunch, place it in a bucket that's about a quarter filled with water so just the bottoms of the stems get wet. This will keep the plants fresh until you're ready to dry them.

Don't pile bunches on top of one another if you can help it, as they can be easily crushed. If you're short of space or buckets, lay the bunches out flat if possible.

Most things can be rubber-banded together in small bunches for hang-drying, which is the easiest drying method (see the next chapter). However, in some cases, you might want to remove the petals of fleshier flowers, like marigolds and roses, as you gather them. We fill large baskets with petals as we go. If you're picking delicate, whole flower heads, cut them just under the calyx (the outermost floral parts, which are usually green), and place them on flat baskets in a single layer, blossom heads facing up.

The same flower may be gathered and sorted several different ways, and the gathering will be easier if you know this in advance. Take peonies, for example.

We pick them with the stems intact, placing big bunches of them in water buckets as we cut. Then we separate them into three groups. If the heads are full-blown, we'll pull them apart and dry the petals only. These will be used for potpourris and sachets. The most perfect peony heads will be clipped beneath the calyx and later dried in silica gel for use whole on top of potpourris, or in flower wreaths or baskets. The remainder will be hang-dried on their stems and used in flower arrangements and bouquets.

If I don't know what I'll be using something for, I usually keep the flower head and stem intact and hang it to dry. The dried petals can always be used later for potpourri. We do this with our lavender, removing whatever flower heads we need for sachets after all the lavender is hang-dried.

If you're not a very experienced gardener, go through gardening books for more detailed advice on harvesting specific species of plants. Just be judicious. Don't harvest everything at once. Experiment by doing several batches at a time to see how they turn out.

The children gather flowers and herbs early in the morning.

Above and opposite: *Freshly picked flowers and herbs. After it's gathered, the harvest is then ready to be separated and prepared for drying.*

9
DRYING & STORING

After selecting and gathering your summer flower harvest, you'll be ready to preserve its beauty for the coming winter months by drying it. Of course, you can buy already dried materials from botanical suppliers and herb shops, but by drying your own, you have the opportunity to preserve flower varieties and colors that may not be available in the marketplace. Whether you grow your own or buy fresh from a florist, the drying techniques are the same.

The principle of drying flowers is to remove the moisture from them while retaining their original shape and color. Some flowers will come through the process better than others. Colors of certain flower petals and leaves change when they're dry; some dark red or purple flowers tend to dry almost black, while certain white flowers may dry to a dark ivory or brown. Leaves, too, may lose their nice green color as they lose moisture. So keeping this in mind, use as a guide the lists of botanicals in Chapter 8 —at least when you're starting out. After that, you'll probably want to experiment with different varieties to see how they weather the drying process.

I use five different methods for drying: hang-drying, air-drying, oven-drying, water-drying, and silica gel. Employing these methods, I dry things as they become available all spring and summer long. Even in fall and early winter there will be things that you will want to preserve.

The drying process is a time-consuming one in which patience and a degree of delicacy are called for. You should have a place in the kitchen, garage, or a shed where you can work without distractions and have your knife, scissors, string, rubber bands, and other drying supplies at hand.

Whatever method you use, your flowers should be placed in a well-ventilated room with good air circulation and low moisture, away from heat. Attics, big closets, or a garden shed would all serve the purpose. Good air circulation will ensure that your flowers dry as quickly as possible, which will result in better color preservation and cut down on the possible growth of mold. Another way to keep colors from fading is to keep all drying materials away from direct sunlight and avoid areas that are dusty.

The first thing everyone wants to know about drying is how long it takes, and the answer is—it depends. Thick, fleshier flowers take longer than thinner, more sparsely petaled ones. Small bunches of leaves dry more quickly than bigger ones. And separated petals will dry more quickly than flower heads. However, since your botanicals must be bone-dry before you use them in any project, I recommend the following guidelines: correctly dried flower heads and petals should be crisp (like cornflakes), not sticky to the touch. The leaves should crackle when you touch them. And you should check the progress of the botanicals as they're drying—especially if you're using the silica gel method.

HANG-DRYING

This is the easiest and most effective method for drying almost anything—leaves, flowers, or herbs. Another advantage is that you can dry large quantities of things this way. All hang-drying is done with the stems intact, which makes this method ideal for drying botanicals you want to use in bouquets or arrangements.

The hang-drying method works for almost any botanical, especially leafy herbs and foliage like sage, artemisia, lemon verbena, rose leaves, and tansy; for wild flowers such as goldenrod, loose-strife, and Joe-Pye weed; and for cultivated flowers like globe amaranth, larkspur, cornflower, statice, salvia, nigella, poppy, lavender, and peony.

I use the products of hang-drying for flower arrangements, wreaths, and door

Previous page: Bunches of herbs and flowers hung from the rungs of an old drying rack. For the actual drying process, the rack will be moved indoors.

bouquets. Flower heads and petals can also be removed from the stems after drying and used for potpourris and sachets.

Finding a place to hang-dry your botanicals shouldn't be too difficult. I use several old quilt racks for drying my harvest. You can use a laundry rack, hooks along a beam or wall, or a clothesline hung in an attic or a roomy closet. If the area is limited, or you intend to dry a large quantity of things, you can increase the available space by suspending the stemmed flowers or leaves from hangers and hooking the hangers onto the line.

How to Hang-Dry

1. Harvest your botanicals, leaving the longest stems possible.
2. If drying flowers, strip all leaves from the stems. Otherwise they may shrivel up unattractively as they dry.
3. Gather botanicals into bunches: 3 to 5 stems per bunch for larger varieties, like tansy; 5 or more stems per bunch for smaller varieties. (The more you put in a bunch, the longer it will take to dry.) Be sure that flowers and stems aren't tangled together when you bunch them or they'll dry that way and break when you try to separate them. In some cases, you may want to hang them singly, as I sometimes do with marigolds, peonies, and roses.
4. Fasten each bunch together at the end with a rubber band, about 1 inch in from the tips. Rubber-banding is better than tying with string because the rubber band will adjust as the stems shrink during drying and won't fall off. Also, you can easily loop the rubber band over the bar of your drying rack, hanger, or clothesline and then back over the stems, to hang the bunches quickly.
5. Hang the bunches in rows, far enough apart so that they won't tangle or crush each other. Spacing them this way also helps to speed the drying process.

6. If there is dust or too much light in the hanging area, cover each bunch with a paper bag, tying the open top of the bag around the stems with string.

This drying process may take from several days to a week.

OVEN-DRYING

This is a quick method for drying loose petals or thick, fleshy flower heads, but you do have to watch them carefully. It takes less time than air-drying and gives the same effect. In fact, you can oven-dry the same things you would air-dry.

How to Oven-Dry

1. Place separate petals or flower heads on a cookie sheet so that they're one layer deep.
2. Place in a cool (about 100° F.) oven and leave the oven door slightly ajar.
3. Watch the materials carefully until dried.

Depending on what you're drying, the process may take anywhere from a few minutes to several hours.

WATER-DRYING

You may want to try this method for sturdy-stemmed flowers or leaves that you want to dry on the stem. Botanicals dried this way will retain their original appearance even after they've dried, which is why I like to use water-dried materials in my door bouquets, flower arrangements, and wreaths. The result is a more natural look as each stem dries in a random direction just as it has grown.

Water-drying is a good way to dry such flowers as hydrangea, Queen Anne's lace, dock, and baby's breath.

How to Water-Dry

1. Place flowers in a container filled with a small amount of water.
2. Place the container in a warm area out of the sunlight.
3. The water will gradually evaporate, allowing the flowers to dry slowly and look more natural when dried.

Allow several days for drying.

AIR-DRYING

This method is especially convenient for drying lots of loose petals and flower heads for potpourri and sachets. The finished flowers will look as if they dried naturally, as opposed to the "perfect" look you get with silica gel. Flower heads or leaves with stems can also be dried this way. When used in a flower arrangement they add a look of spontaneity.

In order to dry botanicals by this method, you need a flat surface that allows the air to circulate around the drying materials. Window screens, flat baskets, or muslin that's been hung (like a hammock) would all be ideal. Or if you have limited space, you can use a newspaper laid flat on the floor in an out-of-the-way area, such as under a bed or a sofa.

The air-drying method works best for all loose petals, including marigold, cornflower, peony, rose, larkspur, lily, and iris; flower heads such as daisy, zinnia, cornflower, carnation, iris, rose, and violet; single-stemmed flowers such as tulip and peony; and leaves on stems such as rosemary and sage.

Overleaf, left: *Lilacs, tulips, roses, and nigella after being dried in silica gel.*
Right: *Fresh flower heads—lilies, pinks, delphiniums, hollyhocks, and marigolds—in silica gel for drying.*

How to Air-Dry

1. To dry petals, spread them on the flat surface in a single layer in order to hasten drying.

2. To dry flower heads, place them in a single layer in rows, heads facing up.

3. To dry leaves with stems or single-stem flowers, lay them down in a random manner, but don't let them overlap.

The air-drying method may take anywhere from several days to a week.

SILICA GEL

Silica gel is a powdery, sandlike substance that dries flowers in a few days so that they retain good color. The colors usually dry brilliant and clear, and the shapes are preserved in their original state. In fact, flowers dried in silica gel look almost as if they were freshly picked.

Silica gel absorbs moisture from the flowers, and as it does so, the blue dots in the mixture turn pink. When this happens, it means that the maximum moisture content has been reached, and you must dry out the silica gel so that you can reuse it. Simply place it in a baking pan in a 250° F. oven. When the blue color returns, you can use the silica gel again and again. (Silica gel is available at garden centers and florists.)

Less expensive than silica gel is a combination of borax and cornmeal which you can mix yourself. However, I find that the silica is less dusty and more effective, and since it can be used repeatedly, it proves to be more economical in the long run.

Drying with silica gel must be done in covered airtight containers such as rectangular plastic boxes or old dress boxes. You'll want to use this method for drying all flower heads used in wreaths, flower arrangements, and tussie-mussies. I also use silica gel for drying flower heads that

I place on top of potpourris for decoration. This method is good for drying all flower heads, including peony, delphinium, rose, zinnia, anemone, iris, lilac, lily, daffodil, tulip, violet, dahlia, carnation, and calendula.

How to Dry with Silica Gel

Flower Heads

1. Fill the container about one-third full with silica gel.

2. Place the flowers face up in the silica (unless the flowers are flat-petaled varieties like daisy and gerbera, which are best dried face down). Press them gently into the silica gel mixture, making sure that the insides of the flowers are covered with the silica as well. This is necessary in order to retain the original shape of the flower. If you just pour the mixture on top of the flower, it will flatten it.

3. Gently cover the entire blossom with more silica until it's completely covered.

4. Check the flowers every day until they've reached the point when they're dry but not brittle. If you leave flowers in silica gel too long, they'll shatter like glass when you remove them. It takes roughly two to three days for thin-petaled flowers to dry, five to seven days for fleshier flower heads.

5. When the flower is ready, remove it gently with a slotted spoon.

6. If any of the silica gel powder remains clinging to the petals, gently brush it off with a soft, watercolor paintbrush.

7. If any of the petals fall off, just glue them back into place with a drop of clear household glue.

Flowers with Stems

I like to dry some flower heads with wire stems to use later in dried flower arrangements. If you decide to do this, you must first prepare the flower heads before placing them in the silica gel. Here's how:

When drying flower heads for arrangements, leave at least 1 inch of the stem below the calyx. Take a 2-inch length of florist's wire and push it up through the center of the stem. As the flower dries in the silica gel, the stem will shrink over the wire to grip it more firmly. Afterward, when the flower is completely dried, you can twist an additional length of wire onto the original piece to make whatever length stem you need for the flower arrangement.

STORING

Ideally, the storage area for your dried botanicals must meet certain requirements if you don't want all your hard work to go to waste. The area must be dim in order to keep the colors of the flowers and leaves from fading, and it must be cool and dry to discourage the growth of mold.

Translated into practical terms, such an area might be found in a walk-in closet with shelves, or in an old preserves closet, like the one I have in my country house, with lots of room for large baskets and boxes. Another possible storage area would be an attic, which is good for hanging dried materials, especially if there is a window you can open to allow the air to circulate. Just make sure that the light from the window doesn't shine directly on any materials you store there. The garage might be another good alternative if it isn't damp and a heavy-traffic area.

Even apartment dwellers with limited space can find a storage area somewhere. Try investigating the top of a closet in a bedroom. Kitchen shelves in an old butler's pantry would be good, too, if the area is dry and cool. Finally, if your closets and pantries refuse to yield any extra space, you can always find room beneath sofas and beds for storage.

Wherever you decide to store your dried botanicals, the space should be set up so that you don't have to move the containers around too much. Remember, dried ingredients are very fragile and crush easily, so always handle with care.

Dry or moist potpourri is best stored in widemouthed glass jars or crocks with airtight covers. Actually, almost any nonporous container with a top will do, and if you have some glass jars that are tinted or opaque, so much the better.

Dried materials, whether harvested or bought, such as spices or fragrant herbs and flowers, last longer in glass, airtight jars. Nonfragrant flowers and leaves can be stored in shoeboxes, in heavy cardboard or plastic sweater boxes, dress boxes, or in large baskets. Whatever the container, it should have a cover. If you must store the materials in layers, it would be a good idea to separate the layers with tissue paper as an extra precaution against crushing.

Stemmed flowers and leaves can be left bunched together on their drying rack. If you're going to store them in this manner, be sure to cover each bunch with a brown paper bag that's rubber-banded on top to protect against dust and fading.

Flower heads and leaves dried in silica gel can be safely stored in shoeboxes or in plastic boxes with tight tops after lining the boxes with cotton batting or tissue paper. Again, handle these items very carefully when storing, and if you must store in layers within the container, separate each layer from the next with tissue paper. In addition, little sacks of silica gel can be tossed into each container to guard against dampness.

One final reminder: Label everything carefully as you store it. Some spices and petals look very much alike, especially through tinted glass. So to avoid confusion, include the name of the botanical and the date on the label and you'll know what's stored where when you want to use it.

Bunches of peonies hang drying on their stems

Old baskets used to

Baskets of peony and rose petals removed from their stems

Old tinted glass

dry and store the harvest

A preserves closet becomes a storage room for drying

jars of dried botanicals

A country basket filled with dried flowers from the garden

10
A WORKING GARDEN

The first garden we ever planted was an herb garden, and it's been a constant source of joy (and hard work) for us over the years. The benefits of an herb garden are many. Fragrant wreaths and bowls of potpourri fill the house all year long. Herbal vinegars and preserves are put up each summer. But more important, the herb garden is a rallying point for us. Ours is a profusion of leaves and flowers that frames a large stone terrace where we have picnics and parties and entertain friends. Early on summer mornings, we harvest fragrant lavender. On hot afternoons, we relax with sprigs of mint in our iced tea, listening to the buzzing bees and smelling the lemon thyme that's been crushed underfoot between the paving stones on the terrace.

Aside from the esthetic pleasure it's always given us, our garden also provides us with inspiration and many ideas for Cherchez. In that sense it is very much a working garden—an ongoing experiment, constantly changing and expanding as we try new varieties of plants which we think we might enjoy or possibly try out in new products.

Years ago, when customers first started asking us for lavender, we imported it from England and France. However, we were only able to get lavender flowers and many people wanted it on the stem, so we decided to plant some lavender ourselves and were soon delighted to discover how easily and abundantly it grew. Now, we sell it dried in bunches, and people use it massed in bowls and baskets as decoration or in sachets—all fragrant and fresh from our own country garden.

Growing artemisia was another of our experiments. Where once we used to buy it from local farms, we now harvest our own. People love to use it in everything from dried herb wreaths to flower arrangements.

The garden also includes plants like yarrow, tansy, sage, lemon verbena, pot marjoram, and southernwood, which are all put to good use as decoration in our home and in Cherchez.

The herbs in our garden grow alongside a select group of flowers. I like the idea of combining flowers and herbs whenever you can, and I've chosen my flowers so that their colors augment those of the herbs. The flowers, which range from white to pink to fuchsia, include baby's breath, cornflower, delphinium, foxglove, hollyhock, larkspur, scented geranium, statice, pinks, and violet—and whenever they come into bloom, the various shadings of delicate color are glorious.

Over the years we've added new varieties of flowers and herbs, and as the garden grows, so does our delight and enthusiasm. This holds especially true for the very latest of our additions: the roses.

I've always loved roses. They're the quintessential flower ingredient in potpourri, yet we never attempted to grow our own before. The reason is, I think, that the hybrid roses I'd seen in gardens and nurseries had never really appealed to my taste. It wasn't until I'd visited some old-fashioned gardens both here and in

*Roses on a beadwork
and wool needlepoint cushion*

*A fresh tussie-mussie
in a silver posy holder*

*A shrub rose and a fleabane
daisy from the garden*

*A garden of flowers
echoed in antique textiles*

Silica-dried roses lushly arranged in a simple vase

England that I discovered the old shrub roses, or "old roses" as they are sometimes called, the most romantic, free-flowing roses I'd ever seen.

When people think of a rose, most picture a modern hybrid, the kind that's usually found at a florist's, vividly colored and perfect with a long stem. But the old shrub roses are another story. Unlike the hybrids, the flower is fuller-blown and many-petaled in soft, subtle colorations. They range from white and very pale pink to magentas and deep, deep purples that are almost black. Some are striped with pink or purple or fuchsia—almost as though an artist had colored them.

Although most of these roses flower just once a year, I don't consider that a drawback. It makes them even more special, and when they do appear, their flowering is astonishingly profuse, lush, and lavish. Some old shrub roses grow on full bushes that reach over 10 feet in height, their long branches laden with roses that billow gracefully to the ground.

Of all the roses, these are the most fragrant and the ones that really should be used in potpourri. After viewing the gardens at Sissinghurst Castle in England, you come away with the memory of roses —of their beauty and abundance, but most especially of their lovely, haunting scent. There is something very special about the fragrance of these roses, a feeling that was captured by Vita Sackville-West in her *Garden Book:*

Some writers would call it nostalgically scented, meaning everything that burying one's nose into the heart of a rose meant in one's childhood, or in one's adolescence when one first discovered poetry, or the first time one fell in love.

The rose she referred to was one called Souvenir du Docteur Jamain, which she'd found growing against the wall of an old nursery and saved from extinction. She also explains that she was proud of this accomplishment, as well she should have been. For many years

these old roses were neglected, and it was mainly through the efforts of enthusiastic gardeners like her—who found them growing in weed patches or over old wrecks of buildings and salvaged them—that we are able to enjoy their beauty today.

Their history is a long one, and even the names—centifolia, gallica, alba, damask (which is thousands of years old and still grows in Bulgaria where attar of roses comes from today), cabbage, musk, china, and moss—evoke a sense of the past. These are the flowers that you often see printed on beautiful old chintzes and embroidered on old samplers. Many garden writers have compared these roses to old textiles and Ms. Sackville-West says in her *Garden Book* that "some of these traditional roses might well be picked off a Medieval tapestry or a piece of Stuart needlework. Indeed, I think you should approach them as though they were textiles rather than flowers."

Of all the artists and writers who've recorded these roses for us in the past, one of the most famous was Pierre Joseph Redouté. Whenever you come across a watercolor of an old rose reprinted on a postcard or in a book, chances are it was one he painted for the Empress Joséphine when she lived at Malmaison and planted the most extraordinary rose gardens in all of France. Her enthusiasm was so great that she was said to have ordered China-bound French ships to bring new rose seedlings back with them for her.

Over the years many wonderful books have been written about old roses, some of which have become classics on the subject. My favorites include books by G. S. Thomas, Mrs. E. E. Keays, and Gertrude Jekyll (see Suggested Reading). If you are thinking about planting a rose garden, these books will be an inspiration to you.

There are fashions in gardens as there are in just about everything else, and for many years the old shrub roses had gone out of vogue. But thirty or forty years ago they made a strong comeback, and I'm happy to say that they're becoming popular again today. One reason for that popularity (and the explanation for their survival on the whole) is their incredible hardiness. Unlike hybrids which require a lot of care and spraying, the old roses are easy to grow and tolerant of neglect. In the area where I live, which has severe winters, it is possible to grow many varieties satisfactorily. We've just planted our new garden of old shrub roses and they're already flowering beautifully. Here is a selection of what we've planted. All these roses are especially fragrant and recommended for use in potpourri.

Belle de Crécy, an intoxicatingly fragrant gallica whose newly opened buds are deep pink with tints of violet.

Cardinal de Richelieu, a lush, full-petaled gallica that turns from a lovely coppery rose to a rich violet as it matures.

Common Moss, a classic rose that produces a lush, clear-pink flower.

Empress Joséphine, a silvery-pink gallica and one of the most beautiful.

Ispahan, a soft pink damask rose that has a very long flowering period.

Madame Alfred Carrière, a large noisette with petals that are white with pink.

Madame Hardy, a lovely, flat, white damask rose that flowers in clusters.

Madame Louis Lévèque, a hybrid moss that flowers repeatedly. It's a lush, pink/lavender color.

Marie Louise, another of the beautiful old damasks that was raised at Malmaison. It blooms to a deep pink.

Salet, a moss rose whose clear pink flowers bloom repeatedly and whose scent is exotically musky.

Tour de Malakoff, a centifolia which produces a profusion of fragrant blossoms in pink tinged with blue and lavender.

White Rose of York, an alba with a beautiful, loosely petaled white flower; it dates back to the thirteenth century.

Now that the old roses in our garden are coming into bloom, I've gone back to making moist potpourri again, and for the first time, I'm able to use ingredients taken totally from the garden. I find that very satisfying. Also, we're thinking of starting a new line of single-floral essential oils. They'll be done up in special bottles with the petals or buds of the flowers inside—a rose, perhaps.

I love the idea of going back to the past, and I think that's one of the major reasons that the old roses appeal to me as much as they do. The pace of modern life can be exciting, but when I feel overwhelmed by it all, I find myself wanting to go back to a time and place that's quiet and peaceful. For me, the garden and the old roses offer that sanctuary. Their simple beauty and compelling fragrance tend to evoke another, earlier age. And sometimes I think, "I'm smelling the same roses in my garden that Queen Victoria smelled in hers!"

Mine isn't an isolated case, I'm glad to say. There's a wonderful renewal of interest in gardening going on in this country these days, and I can't help believing that a longing to get back to natural things is largely responsible. There's something deeply satisfying about planting a garden and watching it come into bloom—as the confirmed gardeners among you already know. And it doesn't have to end there, because your harvest can be used to create many wonderful, fragrant things for your home. Even if you're unable to have a garden of your own, you can buy natural materials from florists —or forage for them yourself in the countryside. Flowers, herbs, leaves— these natural things are available to all of us and can be a constant source of pleasure throughout the year.

*If the day and night are such
that you greet them with joy
and life emits a fragrance
like flowers
and sweet scented herbs—
that is your success.
All nature is your congratulations.*

—Henry David Thoreau

Source Guide

BOOKS

The following is a list of books by garden writers that I admire. I highly recommend them to anyone who loves flowers and gardening. Although some of them are out of print, you should be able to track them down through your local library or at one of the sources listed under Antiquarian Book Sellers in this guide. Don't forget country book sales either. They are the source of some terrific "finds."

Bardswell, Frances A. *The Herb Garden*. London: A & C Black, 1930.

Berrall, Julia S. *The History of Flower Arrangements*. New York: Viking Press, 1968.

Bloom, Alan. *Perennials for Your Garden*. Chicago: Floraprint, 1981.

Boxer, Arabella, and Philippa Back. *The Herb Book*. London: Octopus Books, 1980.

Bunyard, E. A. *Old Garden Roses*. London: Country Life, 1936.

Coon, Nelson. *Gardening for Fragrance*. New York: Hearthside Press, 1967.

Courtenay, Booth and James H. Zimmerman. *Wildflowers and Weeds*. New York: Van Nostrand Reinhold, 1972.

Edwards, G. *Wild and Old Garden Roses*. New York: Hafner/Macmillan, 1975.

Ely, Helena Rutherford. *A Woman's Hardy Garden*. New York: Macmillan, 1908.

Gault, S. Miller and Patrick M. Synge. *The Dictionary of Roses in Colour*. London: Michael Joseph Ltd., 1985.

Genders, Roy. *The Cottage Garden and the Old Fashioned Flowers*. London: Pleham Books, 1969.

Graves, Eric. *Growing Herbs*. London: Herb Society, 1977.

Greenaway, Kate (illustrated by). *Kate Greenaway's Language of Flowers*. New York: Gramercy Publishing Co., 1978 reprint of 1884 edition.

Griffiths, Trevor. *The Book of Old Roses*. London: Michael Joseph Ltd., Mermaid Books, 1984.

Hemphill, Rosemary. *Fragrance & Flavour*. London & Sydney: Angus & Robertson, 1959.

Jekyll, Gertrude. *Colour in the Flower Garden*. London: Country Life, 1908.

———. *Home & Garden*. London: Longman's Green & Co., 1920.

——— and Edward Mawley. *Roses for English Gardens*. New York: Penguin Books, 1983.

Keays, Mrs. E. E. *Old Roses*. New York: Macmillan, 1935.

Leyel, Mrs. C. F. *The Magic of Herbs*. London: Jonathan Cape, 1926.

Nichols, Beverley. *The Art of Flower Arrangement*. London: Collins Publishing, 1967.

Nicolson, Philippa (edited by). *V. Sackville West's Garden Book*. New York: Atheneum, 1969.

Page, Russell. *The Education of a Gardener*. New York: Random House, 1962 and 1983.

Perenyi, Eleanor. *Green Thoughts*. New York: Vintage Books, 1983.

Pulbrook, Susan and Rosamund Gould. *The Gracious Art of Flower Arrangement*. New York: Doubleday, 1969.

Robinson, William. *The English Flower Garden & Home Grounds*. Edinburgh: The Edinburgh Press, 1883.

Rohde, Eleanor Sinclair. *Rose Recipes*. London: Country Life, 1939.

Sackville-West, Vita. *A Joy of Gardening*. New York: Harper & Row, 1958.

———. *Knole and the Sackvilles*. London: Ernest Benn, 1922.

Scott-James, Anne. *Sissinghurst, The Making of a Garden*. London: Michael Joseph Ltd., 1974.

Sitwell, Sacheverell, Wilfred Blunt, and John Russell. *Old Garden Roses*. London: George Rainbird, 1955–57, two vols.

Spry, Constance. *Constance Spry's Garden Notebook*. New York: Alfred A. Knopf, 1940.

———. *Flowers in House & Garden*. New York: G. P. Putnam, 1937.

Stemler, Dorothy. *Book of Old Roses*. Boston: Bruce Humphries, 1966.

Thomas, Graham Stuart. *Old Shrub Roses*. London: J. M. Dent & Sons, 1955.

Verey, Rosemary. *The Scented Garden*. New York: Van Nostrand Reinhold, 1981.

GARDENS

We love to visit gardens here and abroad, especially in Britain. So here I've listed my favorites. As we live on the East Coast, I've noted those places we've been able to visit easily. This list is not, by any means, all-inclusive. To find out more about special gardens in your area, check with the local Chamber of Commerce or garden clubs.

UNITED STATES

The Abby Aldrich Rockefeller Garden, Seal Harbor, ME, is Chinese-inspired with beautiful flower gardens designed by Beatrix Ferrand, one of our foremost landscape designers.

Arnold Arboretum, Jamaica Plains, MA, is a wonderful place to visit in spring, when over 700 lilac plants are in bloom.

Brooklyn Botanic Garden, Brooklyn, NY. Planted in an Elizabethan Knot design, the herb gardens are among the outstanding ones here.

Dumbarton Oaks, Washington, D.C., also landscaped by Beatrix Ferrand, is especially lovely in spring and fall.

The Farmers Museum, Cooperstown, NY, set within a wonderful group of museum buildings, is a garden filled with medicinal herbs.

Hancock Shaker Village, Hancock, MA. Along with restored Shaker buildings, there is a large herb garden with clearly identified plants.

Huntington Botanical Gardens, San Marino, CA, has one of the most spectacular Japanese gardens in this country.

The J. Paul Getty Museum, Malibu, CA, is an unusual museum with lovely gardens.

Longwood Gardens, Kennet Square, PA, contains some magnificent water gardens and conservatories.

Middleton Place, Charleston, SC, is one of the oldest landscaped American gardens.

The National Herb Garden, Washington, D.C., has old roses and herbs planted in specific gardens.

The New York Botanical Garden, Bronx, NY, features an English rose garden as well as many other wonderful flowers.

Old Westbury Gardens, Old Westbury, NY. The gardens of the former Phipps estate include an English rose garden and an Italian garden.

The Paca Garden, Annapolis, MD, is a restored eighteenth-century garden on two acres in the center of town.

Wave Hill, Bronx, NY, in an especially beautiful setting along the Hudson River, includes an herb garden.

ENGLAND

Claverton Manor, The American Museum in Britain, Bath. An unusual museum (the only American one on foreign soil), with lovely gardens. Small but special.

Exbury, Hampshire, is famous for its miles of rare azaleas and rhododendrons.

Hidcote Manor, Gloucestershire, begun at the turn of the century by Lawrence Johnston and considered one of the most influential gardens in England.

Nymans, West Sussex, covers thirty acres of land filled with magnificent natural gardens and walks, planted by the Messel family.

Sissinghurst Castle Gardens, Kent, offers an intimate, imaginative series of gardens designed by Harold Nicolson and planted by Vita Sackville-West.

Stourhead, Wiltshire, is a "natural" garden —an example of eighteenth-century British landscape design at its best.

Wisley, Surrey, is famous for its lush flower borders and model gardens. Over two hundred acres of wonderful garden ideas.

Rosemary

SHOPS & SUPPLIES

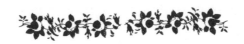

I am a shopper at heart and like to shop in places that have interesting and high quality merchandise, and good service. If they have all three, so much the better! This is my personal list—small but special. Hopefully, you will find everything here that you need to create your own scented rooms.

Although many of the sources are in the Northeast, which is where I live, most will be happy to take mail orders. If you plan to visit, please call ahead as business hours vary and some places are open by appointment only.

HOME FRAGRANCE STORES

This is a list of some of my favorites. All carry a lovely selection of fragrance for the home, including room sprays, scented candles, and the like, in addition to potpourris, sachets, and essential oils. Each has its own particular style and a visit is an experience in itself.

United States

Agraria
1156 Taylor
San Francisco, CA 94108
(415) 771-5922

Caswell-Massey Co., Ltd.
Store:
518 Lexington Ave.
New York, NY 10017
(212) 755-2254

Catalogue Division:
111 Eighth Ave.
New York, NY 10011
(212) 620-0900

Cherchez
862 Lexington Ave.
New York, NY 10021
(212) 737-8215

Crabtree & Evelyn
30 E. 67th St.
New York, NY 10021
(212) 734-1108

England

Culpeper Ltd.
21 Bruton St.
London W1X 7DA
01-499-2406

Czech & Speake
39c Jermyn St.
London SW1 6DN
01-439-0216

Floris
89 Jermyn St.
London SW1 6JH
01-930-2885

Les Senteurs
227 Ebury St.
London SW1 8UT
01-730-2322

Zarvis/London
4 Portobello Rd.
London W10 5T2
01-968-5435

France

Beauté Divine
40 Rue Saint Sulpice
Paris 75006
326-2531

Comptoir Sud-Pacifique
34 Place Marché St.
    Honoré
Paris 75001
261-0676

Diptyque
34 Blvd. St. Germaine
Paris 75005
326-4527

L'Artisan Parfumeur
5 Rue Capucines
Paris 75001
296-3513

Le Saponifère
12 Rond Point Des
    Champs Élysées
Paris 75008
562-3881

Italy

Farmaceutica di Santa Maria Novella
Via della Scala, 16
50123, Florence
21.62.76

DRIED BOTANICALS FOR MAKING POTPOURRI

If you want to order already dried flowers, herbs, spices, and fixatives for making potpourri and sachets, the following stores have them. Each store has a nice selection as well as a price list and/or catalogue.

Aphrodisia
282 Bleecker St.
New York, NY 10014
(212) 989-6440

Caswell-Massey Co., Ltd.
Store:
518 Lexington Ave.
New York, NY 10017
(212) 755-2254

Catalogue Division:
111 Eighth Ave.
New York, NY 10011
(212) 620-0900

Cherchez
862 Lexington Ave.
New York, NY 10021
(212) 737-8215

Country Herbs
Box 1133
Stockbridge, MA 01262
(413) 298-3054

ESSENTIAL OILS

Everyone on this list has what I consider to be good quality, single-essence essential oils. Each has a price list and/or catalogue.

United States

Capriland's Herb Farm
Silver Street
North Coventry, CT 06238
(203) 742-7244

Caswell-Massey Co., Ltd.
Store:
518 Lexington Ave.
New York, NY 10017
(212) 755-2254
Catalogue Division:
111 Eighth Ave.
New York, NY 10011
(212) 620-0900

Cherchez
862 Lexington Ave.
New York, NY 10021
(212) 737-8215

Hové Parfumeur, Ltd.
824 Royal St.
New Orleans, LA 70116
(504) 525-7827

Kiehl's
109 Third Ave.
New York, NY 10003
(212) 475-3400

England

Culpeper Ltd.
21 Bruton St.
London W1X 7DA
01-499-2406

John Bell & Croyden
Department A6 MO
52-54 Wigmore Street
London, W.I.
01-935-5555

FLORIST SUPPLIES AND TOOLS

Floral foam, tape, glue, tools, and silica gel are some of the items available by mail order.

Dorothy Biddle Service
Greeley, PA 18425
(717) 226-3239

DRIED FLOWERS AND HERBS IN BUNCHES

A selection of dried botanicals on stems and forms for making wreaths are available by mail order.

Frank Holder
Box 78, Freedom Rd.
Pleasant Valley, NY 12569
(914) 635-8471

The Herb Farm
Barnard Rd.
Granville, MA 01034
(413) 357-8882

PLANTS, SEEDLINGS, AND SEEDS

The following list includes nurseries that carry live herbs and plants. All will ship them through the mail and have catalogues and/or price lists. A visit is also fun—and informative.

Berkshire Garden Center
Routes 102 and 183
Stockbridge, MA 01262
(413) 298-3926

Capriland's Herb Farm
Silver St.
North Coventry, CT 06238
(203) 742-7244

The Country Garden
Rt. 2, Box 445A
Crivitz, WI 54114
(715) 757-2045

Heirloom Gardens
P.O. Box 138
Guerneville, CA 95446
(707) 869-0967

The Herb Cottage
Washington Cathedral
Mount Saint Alban
Washington, D.C. 20016
(202) 537-8982

Logee's Greenhouses
55 North St.
Danielson, CT 06239
(203) 774-8038

Merry Gardens
Camden, ME 04843
(207) 236-9064

Sandy Mush Herb Nursery
Rt. 2, Surrett Cove Rd.
Leicester, NC 28748
(704) 683-2014

Shady Hill Garden
821 Walnut St.
Batavia, IL 60510
(312) 879-5665

Taylor's Garden
1535 Lone Oak Rd.
Vista, CA 92083
(619) 727-3485

Wayside Gardens
Hodges, SC 29695
(800) 845-1124

Well-Sweep Herb Farm
317 Mt. Bethel Rd.
Port Murray, NJ 07865
(201) 852-5390

White Flower Farm
Litchfield, CT 06759
(203) 567-4565

RARE AND UNUSUAL ROSEBUSHES

You can order the old-fashioned shrub and other rare or miniature roses for your garden from these special nurseries and they will ship them to you. Remember to inquire about permits needed to import from England to the United States.

United States

High Country Rosarium
1717 Downing at Park Ave.
Denver, CO 80218
(303) 832-4026

Pixie Treasures
4121 Prospect Ave.
Yorba Linda, CA 92686
(714) 993-6780

Roses by Fred Edmunds
6235 S.W. Kahle Rd.
Wilsonville, OR 97070
(503) 638-4671

Roses of Yesterday and Today, Inc.
802 Brown's Valley Rd.
Watsonville, CA 95076
(408) 724-3537

England

Peter Beales Roses
London Rd.
Attleborough
Norfolk NR17 1AY
(0953) 454707

GARDENING TOOLS

These companies offer high quality, well-designed gardening tools in addition to related items by mail order.

United States

Gardener's Eden
P.O. Box 7307
San Francisco, CA 94120
(415) 428-9292

Smith & Hawkins
25 Corte Madera
Mill Valley, CA 94941
(415) 383-4050

England

Burgon & Ball Ltd.
Retford Rd.
Woodhouse Mill
Sheffield S13 9WJ
South Yorkshire.
0742-690881

ANTIQUARIAN BOOKSELLERS

These people specialize in antique, rare, and out-of-print books on landscape gardening, fragrance, herbs, flowers, horticulture, flower arranging, garden ornaments, architecture, and garden history. Each has a catalogue.

K. Gregory
222 E. 71st St.
New York, NY 10021
(212) 288-2119

Timothy Mawson Books
New Preston, CT 06777
(203) 868-0732

John H. Stubbs
28 E. 18th St.
New York, NY 10003
(212) 982-8368

Robin Wilkerson Books
24 Groveland St.
Auburndale, MA 02166
(617) 969-2678

Elisabeth Woodburn
Booknoll Farm
Hopewell, NJ 08525
(609) 466-0522

ANTIQUE BOTANICAL PRINTS, DRAWINGS, AND ENGRAVINGS

These people stock a wonderful selection of lovely old prints on botanical or related subjects, such as gardens,

architecture, and interior design. Most have catalogues.

United States

Florilegium
Oriel Eaton Kriz
Box 157
Snedens Landing
Palisades, NY 10964
(914) 359-2926

K. Gregory
222 East 71st St.
New York, NY 10021
(212) 288-2119

Jutta Buck
4 East 95th St.
New York, NY 10128
(212) 289-4577

Timothy Mawson Books
New Preston, CT 06777
(203) 868-0732

Pageant Book & Print Shop
109 East 9th St.
New York, NY 10003
(212) 674-5296

The Old Print Shop
150 Lexington Ave.
New York, NY 10016
(212) 683-3950

John H. Stubbs
28 East 18th St.
New York, NY 10003
(212) 982-8368

Ursus Prints
39 East 78th St.
New York, NY 10021
(212) 772-8787

England

Stephanie Hoppen
17 Walton St.
London SW3 2HX
01-589-3678

The Print Room
37 Museum St.
London WC1A 1LP
01-430-0159

Lantern Gallery
9 George St.
Bath BA1 2EH
(0225) 63727

INDEX

Note: Page numbers in *italics* refer to illustrations.

A

Air-drying, 21, 28, 92, 105, 108
Alcohol, in floral waters, 49
Apples, for pomanders, 48
Aromatic diffusers, 61
Artemisia, *90–91,* 113
    in wreaths, 68, *70*
Attar of roses, 13

B

Bardswell, Frances A., 93
Basil, 68, *70,* 73
Bath Bags, 37, *39*
Bergamot oil, in Florida Water, 52
    in Scent Pillows, 41
    in Travel Sachets, 36
Black-eyed Susans, *95*
Blue malva, *11*
Boiling spices, 49
Books, 121, 127. *See also specific titles*
Borage, *95*
Botanicals, dried, sources of, 125
Bottles, lavender, 45, 52–53, *54–55*
Bouquets
    door, 73, 76–77, *78–79*
    equipment and materials for, 76, 127
    tussie-mussies, 73, *74–75,* 76, *114,* 127
Bowls
    for displaying potpourri, 24, *30–31*
    for making potpourri, 16, 28

C

Candles, scented, 57, *58*
    61
Cedar shavings, *11*
Chamomile
    in Herbal Water, 51
    Roman, *11,* 16, *18*
Cherchez's Old English

Rose Potpourri, 16, *18,* 20
Cinnamon, powdered, 17
Cinnamon sticks, *11*
    boiling, 49
Citrus Potpourri, 21, *22–23*
Closet Door Bouquet, 77
Cloves, *11*
    boiling, 49
    in Florida Water, 52
    for pomanders, 48, 49
Cologne, 13
Color, preserving, 101, 108, 109
Constance Spry's Garden Notebook (Spry), 84
Containers
    for displaying potpourri, 24, *30–31*
    for flower arrangements, 85
    for making potpourri, 16, 25, 28
    for storing, 109, *110–11*
Cottage Garden Potpourri, 21, *22*
Curing spice mixture for pomanders, 48–49

D

Delphiniums, *107*
Diffusers, aromatic, 61
Door bouquets, 73, 76–77, *78–79*
Drawer liners, 60
Drawings, sources of, 127
Drying, 101
    air-, 21, 28, 92, 105, 108
    hang-, *102–3,* 104–5, *110, 111*
    for moist potpourri, 28
    orange peels, 21
    oven-, 105
    silica gel, *106–7,* 108–9
    water-, 105
Dry potpourri, 13, *14–15, 18–19, 22–23. See also* Drying
    equipment and materials for, 16, 125–26
    recipes for, 17, 20–21

refreshing, 24–25
to store, 109

E

Eau de cologne in potpourri, 13
Education of a Gardener, The (Page), 93
English Flower Garden and Home Grounds, The (Robinson), 96
Engravings, sources of, 127
Equipment and materials
    for bouquets, 76, 127
    for drying plants, *102–3,* 104, 105, *110–11*
    for flower arrangements, 85, 127
    for gathering plants, 97
    for making pomanders, 48
    for making potpourri, 16, 25, 28, 125–26
    for making wreaths, 68, 69, *70–71,* 127
    sources of, 125–27
    for storing, 109, *110–11*
Essential oils, 12–13, 57, 60. *See also specific oils*
    aromatic diffusers for, 61
    in Powder Sachets, 40
    refreshing dry potpourri with, 24–25
    refreshing sachets with, 40
    sources of, 13, 126
    in wreaths, 68
Eyedroppers, 16

F

Fabrics for sachets, 35
Fireplace scents, *58–59,* 60
Fixatives, 12. *See also specific fixatives*
    sources of, 125
Floral waters, 45, 49, *50, 51*
    recipes for, 51–52
Florida Water, 52

Florist supplies, sources
   of, 126
Flower(s), 12. *See also*
   Petals; *specific flowers*
   arranging, 81, *82–83,*
      84–85, 127
   bouquets, 73, *74–75,*
      76, *114–15*
   in Cottage Garden
      Potpourri, 21, *22*
   dried, preserving color
      in, 101, 108, 109
   dried, sources of, 126
   to dry. *See* Drying
   gathering, 96–97, *99*
   growing, 113, 116–17
   meaning of, 77
   selecting, 89, 92–93
   sources of, 125–27
   to store, 109
   wild, 92–93
   wreaths, 65, *66–67,* 69,
      71, 127
Foxglove, *94*
Fruit for pomanders, 48

G

Garden Book (Sackville-
   West), 116
Gardening, 93, 96, 113,
   116–17
   tools for, sources of, 127
Gardens to visit, 123
Gathering plants, 96–97,
   99
Geraniums, rosebud, *106*

H

Hang-drying, *102–3,* 104–
   5, *110*
Heather, *18–19*
Herb(s), 12. *See also*
   specific herbs
   in arrangements, 85
   bouquets, 73, 76–77, *78–*
      79
   dried, sources of, 126
   to dry, *102–3,* 104
   gathering, 96–97, *99*
   growing, 93, 113
   pillows. *See* Scent
      Pillows
   in potpourri, 17, 20, 21, 29

in sachets, 35–37
   selecting, 93
   sources of, 125–27
   to store, 109
   Water, *50,* 51
   wreaths, 65, 68–69, *70,*
      127
Herb Garden, The
   (Bardswell), 93
Hibiscus, *11*
Hidcote lavender, *95*
Hollyhocks, *107*
Home and Garden
   (Jekyll), 25
Home fragrance stores,
   125

I

Incense, 57, 61

J

Jekyll, Gertrude, 25
Joséphine, Empress of
   France, 116

K

Kitchen scales, 16
Knole, England, 29

L

Lady Betty Germain's
   Recipe, 29
Lamps, perfume, 57, 61
Larkspur, *91, 94*
Lavender, *11, 95,* 113
   in Bath Bags, 37
   bottles, 45, 52–53, *54–*
      55
   in fireplace, *58–59*
   in Florida Water, 52
   Potpourri, Spicy, *14–15,*
      17
   Sachets, 36, *38*
   Water, 51
Leaves, 12
   to dry, 92, 101, 105, 108
   selecting, 89, 92
   to store, 109
Lemon Furniture Sachets,
   36, *38*
Lemongrass, *11*

Lemon verbena, *11*
   in Lemon Furniture
      Sachets, 36
   Scent Pillow, 41
Lemons, for pomanders,
   48
Leyel, Mrs. C. F., 52
Lilacs, *106*
Lilies, *107*

M

Magic of Herbs, The
   (Leyel), 52
Marigolds, *11, 94, 107*
Materials. *See* Equipment
   and materials
Measuring, equipment for,
   16
Men's Shirt Sachets, 37, *39*
Moist potpourri, 13, 28–
   29, *30–31*
   equipment and
      materials for, 25, 28,
      125–26
   recipe for, 29
   to store, 109
Monkshood, *91*
Mortar and pestle, *10–11,*
   16
Moth Sachets, 36–37, *39*

N

Nigella, *91, 106*
Nurseries, 126–27
Nutmeg, *11*

O

Oakmoss, *11,* 12
Oils. *See* Essential oils
Old English Rose
   Potpourri, 16, *18,* 20
Old roses. *See* Shrub roses
Orange peels, *11*
   in Citrus Potpourri, 21
   to dry, 21
Oranges, for pomanders, 48
Orrisroot, *11,* 12
Oven-drying, 105

P

Page, Russell, 93

Papers, scented, 60, 61
Patchouli, *11*
   in Woodland Potpourri, 20, 37
Peonies, 97, *110*
Perfume lamps, 57, 61
Petals, *110*
   to dry, 28, 101, 104, 105
   in floral waters, 49
   gathering, 97
Pillows, Scent, 40–41, *42–43*
Pine cones, *58–59,* 60
Pinks, *107*
Plants, seedlings and seeds, sources of, 126
Pomanders, 45, *46–47*
   making, 48–49
Potpourri, 9. *See also* Dry potpourri; Moist potpourri; *specific ingredients*
   Cherchez's Old English Rose, 16, *18,* 20
   Citrus, 21, *22–23*
   Cottage Garden, 21, *22*
   equipment and materials for, 16, 25, 28, 125–26
   ingredients for, *10–11,* 12–13
   Lady Betty Germain's recipe, 29
   recipes for, 17, 20–21, 29
   Spicy Lavender, *14–15,* 17
   to store, 109
   Woodland, *18–19, 20*
Powder Sachets, *39,* 40
Prints, sources of, 127

Q

Quassia chips, *11*

R

Redouté, Pierre Joseph, 116
Refreshing
   dry potpourri, 24–25
   sachets, 40
Robinson, William, 96
Roman chamomile, *11,* 16, *18*

Room sprays, 57, 60
Rose(s), *11, 106, 110, 115*
   attar of, 13
   in Bath Bags, 37
   growing, 113, 116–17
   Potpourri, Old English, 16, *18,* 20
   Scent Pillow, Spicy, 41
   shrub (old), *91, 114,* 116–17
   sources of, 126–27
   in tussie-mussies, 76
   Water, 52
Rosebud geraniums, *106*
Rosemary
   in fireplace, *58–59*
   Scent Pillow, 41

S

Sachets, 33, *34, 35, 38–39*
   Bath Bags, 37, *39*
   fabrics for, 35
   Lemon Furniture, 36
   Men's shirt, 37, *39*
   Moth, 36–37, *39*
   Powder, *39,* 40
   recipes for, 35–37, 40
   refreshing, 40
   Travel, 36, *38*
Sackville-West, Vita, 29, 116
Safflower, *11*
Sage, *90–91*
Santa Maria Novella (Florence), 61
Scales for weighing ingredients, 16
Scented candles, 57, *58,* 61
Scented papers, 60, 61
Scent Pillows, 40–41, *42–43*
Seeds, 92, 126
Shirt Sachets, Men's, 37, *39*
Shrub (old) roses, *91, 114,* 116–17
Silica gel, *106–7,* 108–9
Silver King artemisia, in wreaths, 68
Silver Lace Artemisia, *90–91*
Sissinghurst, England, 20, 116, 121, 123
Snapdragons, *91*

Southernwood, in Moth Sachets, 36–37
Spices, 12. *See also specific spices*
   boiling, 49
   for pomanders, 48–49
   sources of, 125
Spicy Lavender Potpourri, *14–15,* 17
Spicy Rose Scent Pillow, 41
Spoons, 16
Sprays, room, 57, 60
Spry, Constance, 84
Storing, 109, *110–11*
Supplies. *See* Equipment and materials
Sweet Cicely, *90–91*

T

Tarragon, *94*
Thoreau, Henry David, *118*
Thyme, *94*
Travel Sachets, 36, *38*
Tulips, *106*
Tussie-mussies, 73, *74–75,* 76, *114,* 127

U

Uva ursi, *11*

V

Villa Foscari, Venice, 9
Vodka, in floral waters, 49

W

Water-drying, 105
Waters. *See* Floral waters
Wild flowers, 92–93
Woodland Potpourri, *18–19, 20*
   in Men's Shirt Sachets, 37
Wreaths
   equipment and materials for, 68, 69, *70–71,* 127
   flower, 65, *66–67,* 69, *71*
   herb, 65, 68–69, *70*